ALSACE AND LORRAINE

FROM CÆSAR TO KAISER
58 B.C.–1871 A.D.

RUTH PUTNAM

Published by Left of Brain Books

Copyright © 2021 Left of Brain Books

ISBN 978-1-396-32039-2

First Edition

All rights reserved. No part of this publication may be reproduced, distributed, or transmitted in any form or by any means, including photocopying, recording, or other electronic or mechanical methods, without the prior written permission of the publisher, except in the case of brief quotations embodied in critical reviews and certain other noncommercial uses permitted by copyright law. Left of Brain Books is a division of Left of Brain Onboarding Pty Ltd.

Table of Contents

FOREWORD	1
ALSACE AND LORRAINE	2
ALSACE	3
I. Romans, Gauls, and Others on the Soil of Alsace	4
II. The Treaty of Verdun and Other Pacts Affecting Alsace	14
III. The Dream of A Middle Kingdom	17
IV. The People of Alsace in the Fifteenth Century and After	23
V. The Thirty Years' War and the Peace of Westphalia	27
VI. Louis XIV. and Strasburg	38
VII. Alsace after Annexation to France	44
LORRAINE	50
I. Racial Elements	51
II. When the Map was in the Making	56
III. The Aspirations of Burgundy	61
IV. The New Learning	66
V. The House of Lorraine in Europe	71
VI. The Last Dukes of Lorraine	82
VII. The French Revolution	86
VIII. The Language	89
ELSASS-LOTHRINGEN	91
I. After the Cession	93
APPENDIX	107
I. The Treaties	107
II. Main Sources Used for the Narrative	111

FOREWORD

THE War of 1914, exciting interest in past problems as well as in a stormy present, has turned the attention of the general public to the make-up of European nations. This is the excuse for giving a large subject short shrift,—it being one that may again be a vital topic. The stories of Alsace and of Lorraine are scattered about on the pages of English histories or told concretely in little accessible foreign literature, and time-pressed readers may find a connected sketch of their evolution convenient. What I have tried to do was to bring a few landmarks on a long road into consecutive line. May they be at least signposts to the more curious.

R. P.

WASHINGTON, D. C.,
December, 1914.

ALSACE AND LORRAINE

DURING forty-three years these two names have been linked together in a neat phrase. Under that verbal yoke they passed, as the result of the fortunes of war, from one political framework to another. But the two applied to distinct entities. The gradual evolution of each into a semblance of unity out of a congeries of private estates and ecclesiastical foundations, the liege lords they acquired or found imposed upon them, mediate or immediate, the resources, characteristics, customs of each belong to different stories, though sometimes, indeed, containing similar chapters. Alsace and Lorraine were alike in being tiny buffer territories, occasionally little more than geographical expressions, wedged between big "interests." Both have suffered as shuttlecocks under blows of battledores from the east and the west. Here are in brief the stories of each.

ALSACE

AS a working basis, the geographical expression ALSACE may be assumed to include a tract bounded by the Vosges Mountains on the west and the Rhine on the east, lying between 47° 30′ north latitude and 49° 15′, more or less. The breadth is always Alsatian; the length varies. Its area is about 3350 square miles, making this debated land about equal in size to Lancashire, rather larger than Delaware and smaller than Connecticut. The plain of Alsace, between the mountains and the Rhine, is well watered by the Ill and its tributaries, whence comes the name, ILL-SASS, ELLSASS, Elsass, the seat of the Ill. When the designation—a very natural local term—was first applied, is not certain. Nor, indeed, is the derivation of land name from river universally accepted. Several writers, since 1870, have read the phrase *Herzöge der Elisassen* as "Dukes of the foreigners"—*Elisassen* being applied by the Franks to the people in the Vosges region who had crossed from the other side of the Rhine, or by the Germans on the right bank to their fellow-countrymen who had already sought homes on the left. Again, Elsass is read as *Edelsass*, meaning either "the land of the nobles" or the "noble site."

The earliest form of designation, *pagus Alsacinse*, found in documents, did not apply to precisely the same tract as the later name. Thus vagueness envelops Alsatian beginnings. But certain events actually happened east of the Vosges Mountains, in the Ill Valley, before it was classed as such, and were described by a Roman eyewitness. With that description this narrative may begin.

I.

ROMANS, GAULS, AND OTHERS ON THE SOIL OF ALSACE

WHEN Julius Cæsar was making his way farther and farther into Gaul, he found strained relations between the inhabitants of Gallic race in the vicinity of "Mons Vosegus"—the Vosges region—and would-be immigrants from over the Rhine. Divitiacus the Æduan tells the Roman general (*De Bello Gallico*, i., cap. xxxi.) that about 15,000 Germans had "at first crossed the Rhine; but after these wild barbarians had become enamoured of the lands and the refinement and abundance of the Gauls, more were brought over, until about 120,000 of them were in Gaul."

How various clans had suffered from this invasion is recounted in the *Commentaries*. Unfortunately most of the readers of that record (immortal in spite of the arrogance and disingenuousness often displayed by the complacent author) do not appreciate that the Æduans and Sequanians were real people, dwelling on the outskirts of other Celtic tribes,[1] of tribes kindred to them, and exposed to the inroads of alien clans of Germanic blood.

It is a pity that a wonderful historic document should be wasted on reluctant immature readers who only read that they may be free to run and are heedless of the contents of the words that they construe laboriously. Very few adults ever recur to a volume associated with dull school work and so an interesting story falls flat.

The Sequanians, Cæsar heard, were particularly disconsolate for

> Ariovistus, the King of the Germans, had settled in their territory, and had seized upon a third of it, the best land in the whole of Gaul; and now he demanded that the natives should vacate another third, because a few months previously 24,000 Harudes had joined him, and he had to find homestead land for them.

---

[1] One version of the international episode that follows is: "The Celts, as always happens with *moribund races*, were divided into two factions, one of which sought Roman protection while the other depended upon the Germans" (*Geschichte des Elsasses*, Ottokar Lorenz and Wilhelm Scherer, Berlin, 1886).

Within a few years, the entire population of Gaul would be expatriated, and the Germans would all cross the Rhine; for there was no comparison between the land of the Germans, and that of the Sequanians, or between the standard of living among the former and that of the latter.[2]

Cæsar was moved to sympathy for these Celtic folk thus threatened by a veritable inundation from the Rhenish valley, and especially for the Sequanians, whose lot was the most pitiable because they were afraid of harsh treatment from the dreaded *rex Germanorum*, if it were known that they complained. "Ariovistus had wrapped himself in so much haughtiness and arrogance that he had become unbearable."

Cæsar was especially wrathy at this behaviour of the German leader because the Æduans, who were among those thus menaced by these inroads of trans-Rhine peoples, had actually been addressed as "Brothers and Kinsmen," by the Roman Senate. Thus the conduct of Ariovistus was a direct insult to himself and to Rome (cap. xxxiii.).

Moreover, altruism apart, Cæsar foresaw that, if the Germans became accustomed to crossing the Rhine and migrating to Gaul in large numbers, there would be danger for the possessions of the Roman people.

> He believed that, being fierce barbarians, they would not stop short when they had taken possession of the whole of Gaul, but would overrun the Province, as the Cimbri and Teutons had done before, and thence push their way into Italy. The Sequani were only separated from our Province by the Rhine; and he deemed it essential to repulse the danger at the earliest possible moment (cap. xxxiii.).

Accordingly, Cæsar proceeded immediately to take measures for self-protection. Ariovistus was already known to him. Indeed the *rex*

---

[2] "Sed pejus victoribus Sequanis quam Æduis victis accidisse, propterea quod Ariovistus, rex Germanorum, in eorum finibus consedisset tertiamque partem agri Sequanis qui esset optimus totius Galliæ, occupavisset et nunc de altera parte tertia Sequanos decedere juberet, propterea quod mensibus ante Harudum milia hominum viginti quattuor ad cum venissent quibus locus ac sedes pararentur. Futurum esse paucis annis uti omnes ex Galliæ finibus pellerentur atque omnes Germani Rhenum transirent; neque enim conferendum esse Gallicum cum Germanorum agro, neque hanc consuetudinem victus cum illis comparandum." (I., cap. xxxi.).

5

Germanorum had had relations with the great Republic and knew something of the world beyond his own boundaries. He had solicited the friendship of Rome when Cæsar himself was Consul and the latter had never dreamed that "the former would abrogate his loyalty so rashly" (cap. xl.).

He found him now really insufferable in his pretensions and was not sorry to feel obliged to give him a lesson. How Cæsar succeeded in gaining as his base Vesontio (later Besançon), thus forestalling Ariovistus, who also had designs on that "largest city of the Sequanians" (cap. xxxviii.); how his legions had a panic because of the terrible reports current of the prowess of Ariovistus and his Swabians (Suevi), and how Cæsar inspired them by his eloquent speech, is a story worthy to be read in full. (caps. xl.–liii.).

In his harangue to his troops, Cæsar urges the obligation due to allies like the Æduans, and the duty owed to Rome. He ends by declaring that if the main body of the army is not to be trusted (there had been many signs of disaffection) he would take the tenth legion alone and conquer the oncoming foe, without fear that the dreaded Germans would repulse his trained soldiers. "Upon the delivery of this speech, the minds of all were changed in a surprising manner and intense zeal and eagerness for prosecuting the war were aroused" (cap. xli.).

Before the forces meet, however, Ariovistus suggests that a preliminary conference might clear up the *casus belli*, and Cæsar consents to a colloquy— "he began to think that he [Ariovistus] was now returning to a rational state of mind" (cap. xlii.).

But Ariovistus is perfectly clear in his statements and they are not what Cæsar counts "rational." He will not acknowledge that Cæsar has the slightest justice in the claim that he is simply doing a Roman's duty in espousing the cause of a weak ally of the great Republic. The German asserted stoutly that he had crossed the Rhine,

> not of his own accord, but in response to the invitation of the Gauls, that he had only left home because of the inducements offered him; that his settlements in Gaul had been granted by the Gauls themselves;—that he took by right of war the tribute that conquerors are accustomed to impose on the conquered, that he had not made war on the Gauls but the Gauls on him.

He added that the combined states of the Gauls had been defeated easily by him in a single battle and he was ready to give them another chance, but if they chose peace without the battle it was silly of them to think they could escape the tribute.

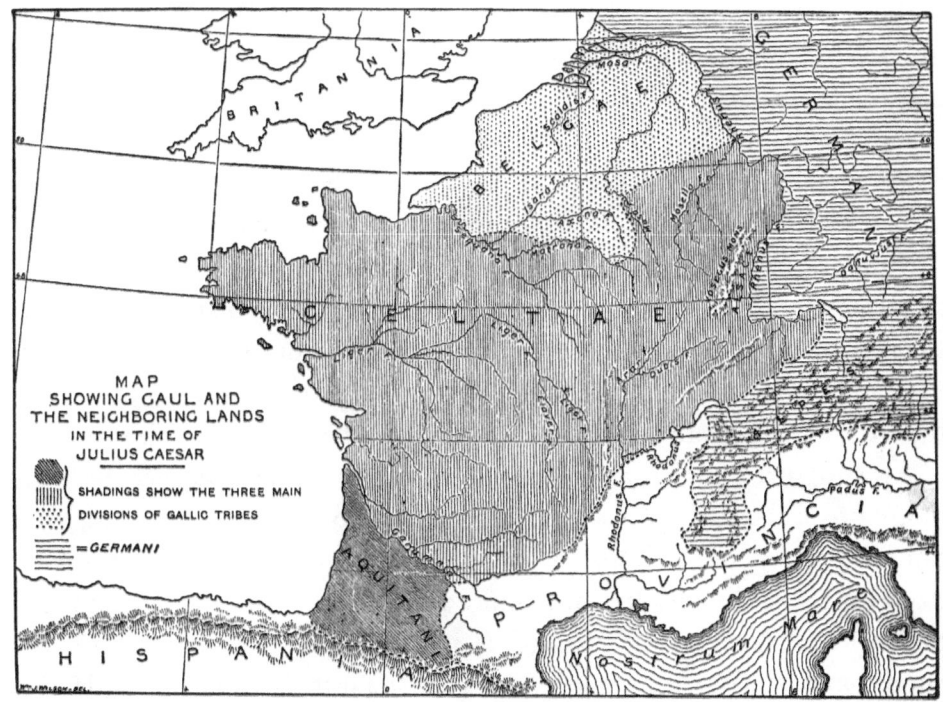

MAP NO. 1
All Gaul Divided into Three Parts.

Furthermore, he said that it would be very pleasant for the Germans to enjoy the friendship of the Roman people, but hardly advantageous if the latter supported the Gauls in refusing tribute, justly his due. He did not lay great stress on the fraternal appellation bestowed by the Senate upon the Æduans, for he was not so ignorant of affairs as not to know that in the late hostilities with the Allobrogians, the Æduans had not assisted the Romans, and that in the conflict waged by the Æduans with himself and with the Sequanians, the Æduans had not had the benefit of Roman aid. He was inclined to suspect that Cæsar, under the mask of friendship for down-trodden allies, was keeping his forces in Gaul for purposes directly hostile to the Germans (cap. xliv.).

There was much more of the speech. Ariovistus further declined to admit that the Romans had any business at all in Gaul beyond the pale of their own province. He had been there long before the legions had thought of coming. Cæsar would be wise if he retreated at once. If he refused he must take the consequences. Moreover the *rex Germanorum* knew something of the state of the political parties in Rome. Were he to kill Cæsar sorrow would not be universal. "Some of the nobles and leading men would be pleased." Of that he had ample assurance.

Naturally this attempt to show his relations with domestic factions inimical to Cæsar did not endear the German to the Roman. That part of the discourse, Cæsar did not answer. Or at least he does not give any report of it.

In reply to the advice to go away and leave Ariovistus in possession of the field, thereby winning him as a valuable ally, Cæsar says that it is impossible for him to waive the matter; that it is neither his practice nor that of the Roman people to abandon meritorious allies and certainly he did not consider that Ariovistus had any more right in Gaul than the Roman people (cap. xlv.).

He supported this last assertion with references to the earlier achievements of Quintus Fabius Maximus. He might have prolonged the conference, had it not been whispered to him that some of the hostile troops were throwing stones at his soldiers, so he cut it short and returned to his own camp. The meeting took place on the plain of Alsace,[3] about halfway between the two encampments. Thus it may be counted as the introduction of that land to modern history.

When Cæsar rejoined his legions, he found public opinion changed. To a man all were now ready to engage with the once-feared enemy. The arrogant claims of the Germans excited so much indignation that there was no further manifestation of reluctance to join battle with the invaders from across the Rhine (cap. xlvi.).

We do not know what report Ariovistus sent home either of the conference or the battle that ensued in a few days. It was not immediately decisive. "Although the foe were routed on the left wing and put to flight, they [continued] to press on our men from the right wing with the great number

---

[3] At least that is where a recent authority places it with good reason from the text. Vesontio, the city with the Doubs encircling it, as though described by a compass, is there today in the modern Besançon as our guide. Then there are the Vosges Mountains and the Rhine as enduring landmarks. See Thomas Rice Holmes, *Cæsar's Conquest of Gaul*, pp. 627 *ff.*, London, 1899,

of their troops." But at last when "the engagement was renewed, all the enemy turned their backs, nor did they cease to flee until they reached the Rhine, about fifty miles from that place."

Ariovistus escaped alive and crossed the river, losing, however, two wives in his flight. Trans-Rhine migration was checked for a time. The Suevians were already on their way westward to reinforce Ariovistus when the news of this disaster reached them and they turned around and went home (cap. liv.).

Undoubtedly the arena in which this Romano-German conflict was decided lay well within Alsace. The two camps are located by scholars between the Fecht River and the foothills of the Vosges, between the present Zellenberg and Ostheim, the German on the west, the Roman on the east, and the line of Ariovistus's retreat was north-east to a point on the Rhine near modern Schlettstadt.[4] It was not, however, the first time that border hostilities had occurred in the Rhineland. Cæsar's own narrative implies a series of similar encounters as having already taken place in the neighbourhood, where the pleasant arable land tempted seekers for subsistence from over the river. The Seat of the Ill entered upon its destiny.

Cæsar spent the winter of 58–57 B.C. in the Roman province and in the following summer opened operations against those Gallic tribes that were still outside of the protection of the Roman eagle. He found a strange reluctance to accede to his natural desires to teach them the rudiments of Latin civilization. Among all the Gauls he found the Belgians to be the bravest,—*horum omnium fortissimi sunt Belgæ.* His long-drawn-out battles on the Axona—the Aisne—and the Sabis—the Sambre—are the precursors of centuries of clashes of arms in those river valleys. It was a hard task to reduce the Belgæ, because by living in the vicinity of the Germans they had been trained to skill and endurance. It was a vicinity that had forced upon them continuous warfare. But the Roman conquest was accomplished at last in Belgian and in the rest of Celtic land, and then was extended over the Rhine until the barbarian tribes were so interwoven with the Roman legions that it was hard to distinguish between them. Ruins of monuments planned by Romans and constructed by barbarian labour are scattered over Western Europe to tell the tale of who built, who saw, and who destroyed.

---

[4] See Holmes, *Commentaries*, p. 38.

In Alsace, the earliest ruins are not, however, these. There are still traces of preceding occupation. Parts of a great wall, the so-called *Heidenmauer*, are to be seen on the Odilienburg, showing how primitive people of the Vosges highlands tried to protect themselves against assault. Then there are many Druid remains, some near the sites of the Roman temples which are found in considerable numbers. Of Latin theatres, arches, aqueducts, such as blossomed in many parts of Gaul, there are no examples in Alsace. Fortifications and highways, however, remain to prove that the Romans did not neglect the Vosges region.

Argentoratum followed by Strasburg, was one of the Roman strongholds which has never ceased to be a fortified place.

The splendid military roads show the best work of the Romans in this section of their domain. Certain of these can be seen on the so-called Peutinger map of *circa* 200 A.D.[5] Some of the most important ran from Besançon (to use modern terms) to Strasburg, on to Mayence, to Ell, Breisach, and on to the Rhine, from Brumath to Saverne and Metz, from Alsace into Lorraine through the valley of Schirmeck, from Alsace into Lorraine through the valley of the Villi, and in many other directions. If the Peutinger map be rightly dated, many of these highways were later than 200 A.D. But on it can be seen three highways leading out of Strasburg,—*Argentoratum*.[6]

The end of the Gallo-Roman period came imperceptibly. Roman domination simply ceased to exist, and officials of northern race who had administered affairs in the name of Rome continued to hold sway without respect to trans-Alpine authority. German settlement, pre-eminently Frankish and Teutonic, in the Vosges tract westward of the Rhine was not the result of decisive conquest. It was merely gradual trans-Rhenish migration, not differing radically from the kind that had been inaugurated by Ariovistus and checked by Julius Cæsar, except that it was less aggressive and in smaller numbers. The Celtic inhabitants were neither entirely dispossessed nor enslaved by the German colonists, to whom, moreover, they did not remain antagonistic. This must be taken into account in

---

[5] See Map II.
[6] Schöpflin counts this as a Celtish word, Romanized. It means a *ford*.

attempting to arrive at any conclusion as to the ultimate racial status of the Alsatian tract.[7]

Whether in the course of the centuries before 800 A.D. the predominant element remained as essentially Gallo-Frankish, with the characteristics of activity, enterprise, energy, independence, irony, and badinage ascribed to the people of the French realm, as it finally took shape, or whether an inherent Teutonic quality continued to differentiate the Alsatians from their French neighbours on the other side of the Vosges, remains a moot question. The conclusion reached seems to vary according as the writer publishes his volume in Paris or Berlin.

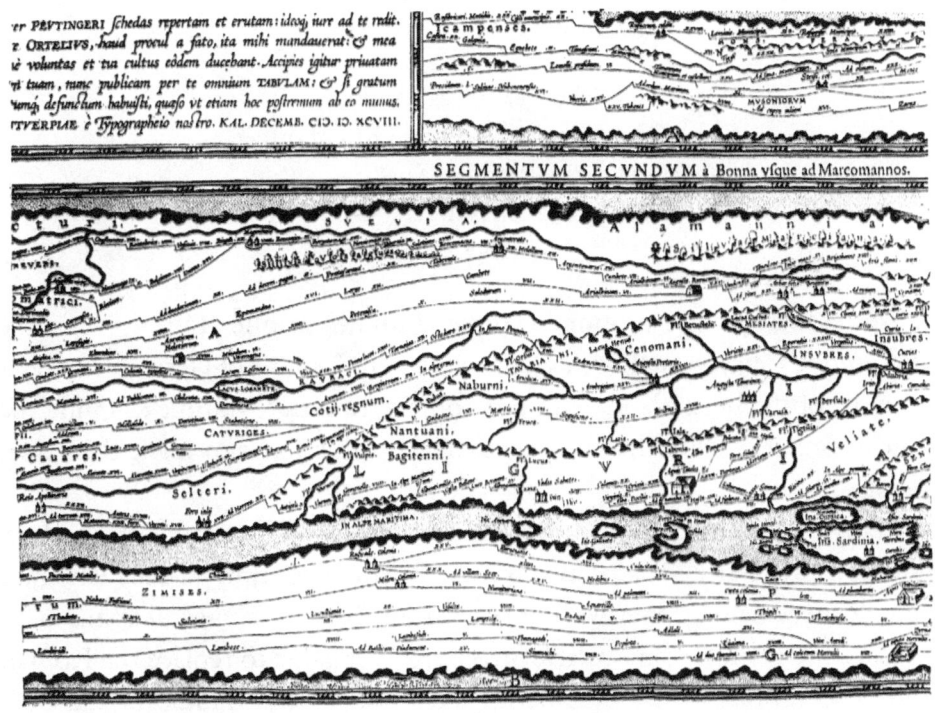

MAP NO. 2
A Section of the Peutinger Map, C. 200 A.D. Territory of Alsace is Between the "Silva Vosagus" and the Rhine. Suevia is on the Other Side of the River.

---

[7] See Schmidt, Charles, *Les seigneurs, les paysans, et la propriété rurale en Alsace*, Paris, 1897.

As far as geographic nomenclature is concerned, it must be conceded that the dominant note in the formative period was Germanic. Strasburg, Breisach, Ebersheim, Rouffac, Seltz, Ell-Sass, itself, however spelled at different epochs, all tell one story, and they are not names that have changed radically during the last phase of political affiliation. But looking at the question in the light of today it must be noted that two fervently French-hearted modern Alsatian writers bear such names as *Kaeppelin* and *Schmidt*.[8] And these are typical of others. Spirit and etymological form do not invariably go hand in hand.

The conclusion seems safe that out of many composing elements two or even three distinguishable currents of lineage, of customs, of language, have had a continuous existence in the make-up of Alsace.

> Drey Schlösser auff einem Berge,
> Drey Kirchen auff einem Kirchhoffe,
> Drey Stätte in einem Thal,
> Ist das gauze Elsass überall—
> [Old German]

"Three castles on one mountain, three churches in one churchyard, three cities in one valley,—such is Alsace, everywhere." This old-German rhyme is symbolic of the borderland, with newcomers from time to time claiming the right to preserve what they had brought with them and to plant their own customs.

Many of those that passed over Alsatian soil did not trouble themselves, indeed, to leave any constructive trace of themselves, though they left trace enough of the damage they wrought. After the Burgundians came Attila, who destroyed Argentoratum—where Strasburg later came to replace the Roman city—and various other settlements. That was in the middle of the fifth century, not long before the invaders were repulsed at Châlons (451 A.D.) by Romans and Germans fighting as allies. Attila went on to Italy and gradually the Alsatians stole down to the plains from the highlands where, like other Gauls, they had taken refuge, and took up their life again amidst the ruins of

---

[8] This applies to Charles Schmidt only. Adolf Schmidt writes on Alsace from a German viewpoint.

the Roman civilization, which had indeed retreated, but which had left a permanent impress upon the land between the Rhine and mountains.

There came a time when the Frankish sovereigns of Gaul recognized the individuality of the province so far as to create a duke of Alsace, and we hear of one Ettich or Attich as bearing that title before Christian times. Legends have clustered about his daughter Odilia, who brought bitter disappointment to her father at her birth, because she was not only a girl when he had desired a boy, but blind at that. The water of baptism finally gave her sight, and the Odilienberg, where she grew up, away from her father's unfriendly eyes, remains to bear witness to the miracle of her conversion to Christianity. The Bishop of Strasburg, too, comes upon the scene and Alsace thus becomes a duchy and has a bishopric, is Christian and provincial. There are many more legends of the region besides those relating to Odilia, but the fascinating suggestions of myth and saga must be left; they belong to another field than that covered by a simple Alsatian chronicle.

Had this title of duke not come into being there might never have been an *Alsace*, but the name persisted even though the unit was fractured.

II.

THE TREATY OF VERDUN AND OTHER PACTS AFFECTING ALSACE

THE Treaty of Verdun, 843 A.D., between the three grandsons of Charles the Great (Charlemagne seems far more befitting that sovereign) gave to Charles the Bald the nucleus of present-day France, to Louis the German, trans-Rhine territory as far as the River Elbe, while to Lothaire, eldest son and Emperor, fell a middle realm between the two familiar divisions of modern Europe. It was *Lotharii regnum*, a realm which bequeathed to posterity one legacy in the name *Lotharingia, Lothringen, Lorraine*, and another in the phantom of an ideal kingdom. One bequest was permanent, though applied to units of different area, the other intermittent in vitality. Modern Lorraine, Alsace, Burgundy, Provence, and Italy, excepting the States of the Church, were all comprised within Lothaire's heritage, in addition to the imperial title. But that allotment was of brief duration. Lothaire II. succeeded his father, indeed, but on his death, his uncles, Charles the Bald and Louis the German, took it upon themselves to make a fresh division of the Carolingian empire into only two parts as far as Europe north of the Alps was concerned.[9] The son of Lothaire II. was permitted to retain the Italian provinces alone of the paternal "Middle Kingdom," while the remainder was parcelled out between his great-uncles, thus marking the confines of France, Germany, and Italy, or rather indicating those three geographical unities. Moreover, not only did modern European boundary lines cast their shadows before at the crises of these territorial divisions but an interesting evidence of the linguistic scission between the subjects of the Frankish sovereigns remains as one result of these fraternal bargains. This is the document containing the oaths sworn at Strasburg, 842 A.D., as a prelude to the formal triangular convention at Verdun, the following year. The two younger brothers safe-guarded themselves against their senior by interchanging pledges of mutual support. The occasion was a formal and solemn function. The brothers were accompanied by their armies, who were taken into their confidence, each overlord addressing his own soldiers in their own vernacular,

---

[9] Freeman points out that each sovereign was still "King of the Franks."

explaining the reasons for enmity towards Lothaire, and then proceeding to give the formal oath each to the adherents of his brother, Louis the German speaking in the *lingua romana*, the speech of Romanized Gaul, and Charles, sovereign of the same realm, using the *lingua teudisca*, spoken across the Rhine. The phrases that were comprehensible to these ninth-century French and Germans look like a very queer jumble of words. Their interest lies in the fact that both vernaculars were probably comprehensible to the bystander in Strasburg, just as the two more polished languages have been in our day. It is probable that thus early the children of the borderland had their ears attuned to bi-lingual addresses. The words of Louis were:

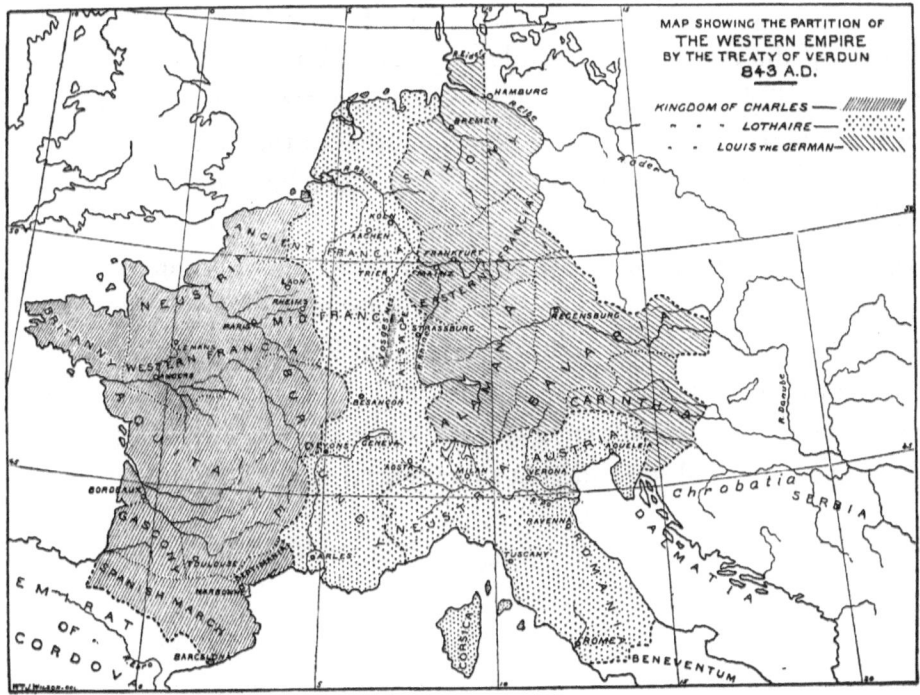

MAP NO. 3
Based on the Map in Freeman's Historical Atlas.

Pro Deo amur et pro christian poblo et nostro commun salvament, dist di in avant, in quant Deus savir et podir me dunat, si salvaraeio cist meon fradre Karlo et in adiudha et in cadhuna cosa, si cum om per dreit son fradra salvar dist, in o quid il mi altresi fazet; et ab Ludher nul plaid numquam prindrai, qui meon vol cist meon fradre Karle in damno sit.

The form of Charles's oath was:

> In Godes minna ind in thes christianes folches ind unser bedhero gealtnissi, fon thesemo dage frammordes, so fram so mir Got gewizci indi madh furgibit, so haldih tesan minan bruodher, soso man mit rehtu sinan bruodher scal, in thiu, thaz er mig sosoma duo; indi mit Ludheren in nonheiniu thing ne gegango the minan willon imo ce scadhen werhen.[10]

The burden of the carefully prepared declarations was that neither party of the compact would damage the other by dealing with Lothaire but each stood pledged to "treat this my brother" as befits fraternal relations, provided "that he does the same by me."

The actual division between Louis and Charles of Lothaire's "Middle Kingdom" did not take place until many years after the Treaty of Verdun. It was not until about 870 that Louis the German entered into the possession of his share, which included Alsace as well as other of the Lotharingian parcels. Then the Vosges Mountains, instead of the Rhine River, became the boundary between the Germanic and Frankish kingdoms. According to a German writer, the *Silva Vosagus* and *Silva Marciana* then entered into their appointed tasks of standing sentinels before the German portal. Germany counted her own birthday as the day when the Treaty of Verdun was signed. A thousand years of existence was celebrated in 1843. Into that thousand-year nationality, Alsace did not enter either at the beginning or the end. On both days her fate was linked to another sovereignty.

---

[10] Emerton, *Mediæval Europe*, p. 27.

III.

The Dream of A Middle Kingdom

HAD the realm covered by the titular authority of Charles the Great remained intact, the Alsatian tract might have had a different history, for the great Carolingian made Colmar and Schlestadt his residence from time to time, and a mid-European capital might have grown into importance,—a capital looking east and west over a wide imperial domain. But after 870 A.D. the lot of Alsace as a border land on Germanized territory was practically decided, although confusing changes continued to make her ultimate political affiliations look very uncertain from time to time. The trail of hazardous fortune cannot be followed in detail. In the twelfth century her fealty was due to the great German King and Roman Emperor (1152),[11] Frederick Barbarossa, while her immediate control was in the hands of various lesser authorities. A new power was springing into being at that period, destined to affect European life more than was possible for the sovereign, seldom seen by the people at large.

That was the free city, waxing into prowess by means of valuable privileges bought from emperors who wished to obtain money for schemes of conquest or personal ambition, or bestowed by them voluntarily for the purpose of erecting burgher bulwarks against over-powerful nobles. In course of time, ten of these communes came into being in Alsace, while Strasburg besides being a city state continued to exert influence as a dominant episcopal see. Long before the two Pragmatic Sanctions of Frederick II. (1220 and 1232) endowed bishops and nobles with supremacy in their own towns,—except when the Emperor was present in person,—this Alsatian bishopric had acquired territorial independence and a high degree of temporal power. Once, indeed, when the city attempted to use influence in an imperial election, it suffered seriously at the hands of the successful candidate whom it had opposed to no

---

[11] For the relation between German King and Roman Emperor, see Bryce, *The Holy Roman Empire*, chap. xiii.

purpose, but as a rule it managed to hold its own against any interference from without.

By the third quarter of the fifteenth century, the state of Alsatian administration was as follows. First, it must be noted that after the episode of Duke Ettich—Eticho, Attich—the dukedom does not seem to have been revived as such. Without examining too curiously how it all happened, we find in existence two landgraviates, dividing Alsace into two *gauen*, the Sundgau and the Nordgau, the latter, Lower Alsace, dependent on the see of Strasburg, the former, Upper Alsace, in the hands of the cadet branch of the House of Habsburg. But even these *gauen* were not intact political units. The free cities dotted here and there over the land were ten in number: Haguenau, the seat of the Prefecture or *Landvogtei*, Colmar, Landau, Schlestadt, Wissenburg, Obernheim, Rosheim, Kaysersberg, Turkheim, and Münster au Val[12]—a goodly array of independent petty exceptions to general authority, united, indeed, under their hereditary Prefect of the House of Habsburg, but realizing that they were members of the Empire in their own right, and were entitled to appeal to the Diet against their Prefect. Mulhouse was another free city not under the Prefect; thus exercising a greater degree of independence.

Moreover, there were five counties, that of Ferrette deserving special mention, and twenty-two lesser seigniories, some fiefs of the Habsburgs and others belonging to other overlords, in addition to more than two hundred feudal castles perched on the crests of the Vosges Mountains or dominating the plain, numerous estates of ecclesiastical foundations, and a number of villages and bailiwicks, imperial or dependent on the see of Strasburg.

Financial embarrassments led to a curious commercial transaction in regard to the lands to which the Habsburgs had title. Sigismund of Austria mortgaged his rights to Charles of Burgundy and the report made to the latter by Jean Poinsot and Jean Pellet, June 13, 1471, gives a detailed account of the condition of Alsace. Here is the story of what happened and what led to such happening.

The Habsburgs took the title by which they have so long been known from a castle built in the eleventh century by one bishop of Strasburg and his brother Radbod upon the Aar, in Swiss territory, not far from the border of

---

[12] All Alsatian names have two forms. Wherever possible, an English form is used in this text.

Upper Alsace. Tradition has it that Radbod followed his hawk—*Habicht*—into an unknown region and was so much charmed with the beauty of the spot that he decided to build a castle there and, later, named the house *Habichtsburg* from the guide who had led him thither. The longer term contracted, naturally, by easy transition into Habsburg and has held its own to this day. Little by little, the family grew to be one of the foremost in the Empire, and in 1273 its reputation was enhanced by the elevation of Rudolph, Count of Habsburg, to the imperial dignity,—the first of many sons of the race to hold that office, although it did not become the assured perquisite of the Habsburgs until later. It may be added that Radbod and his brother the bishop, Werner, who collaborated in the castle building on the heights of the Wulpelsberg, are alleged to be descendants of Duke Ettich of Alsace. Possibly the tradition originated to account for the partition of the two *gauen* or districts of Alsace between the see of Strasburg and the count of Habsburg. After three centuries of fortunes, more or less fair, we find Frederick III. Emperor, and his cousin the Archduke Sigismund, of the cadet branch, in possession of the Habsburg lands in Tyrol and in various other places, besides being Landgrave of the Sundgau and holding other estates in Alsace. Sigismund did not have a compact principality to administer from his capital, Innspruck, and perhaps that was the reason why he fell into serious difficulties in every direction. The Swiss were very troublesome neighbours. He was in a constant state of border warfare with canton or city, sometimes with both. Finally he was so hard pressed that he saw no way of escape but to buy peace outright from the Swiss. The only block to that scheme was that he was already deeply involved in debt and had no cash on hand. There was a group of princes in Europe at this epoch (1460), Louis XI. of France, Charles of Burgundy, Frederick III. and his son Maximilian, who spent their lives in trying to overreach each other. Frederick could not help his cousin, so Sigismund applied to Louis XI. for assistance, but fear of the Swiss made the King refuse. Then the Archduke went down to the Netherlands with his petition and found Charles more amenable. The reason was plain. Charles was most desirous of uniting his Netherland group of duchies, countships, and seigniories with his two Burgundies, and the territories offered to him by Sigismund lay so as to fill in part of the gap between. The Burgundian's hope of erecting a new edition of a "Middle Kingdom" affected his policy in many respects and never more markedly than in this transaction with Sigismund. The bargain was made. Perhaps the fact that the applicant was pretty close to the Emperor, who alone could turn a duke into a real king, made Charles especially willing to oblige his needy visitor. At St. Omer on May 9th another of the long row of treaties was signed which, without the slightest concern for the will of the inhabitants, disposed of the political control of Alsatian soil. Charles agreed to pay Sigismund ten thousand florins immediately and forty thousand before September 24th in return for the cession of all Sigismund's seigniorial rights in the landgraviate of Alsace, the county of Ferrette, and in certain Rhine towns. If he found himself in possession of means to buy back his landgraviate, Sigismund was to be permitted so to do, provided that he could produce at Besançon *the whole sum at once*, that augmented by all the outlays made by the Burgundian upon the property. There were to be no payments on the instalment plan and Charles did not feel much concern lest he should lose the lands thus given over to his complete control. He knew the Habsburg he had to deal with and the prospect that the impecunious Archduke would find fifty thousand and more florins to enable him to redeem Alsace, was very slight. The ten thousand florins promptly paid were used to appease the Swiss and Charles shortly afterwards took steps to enter on his annexed land. Among the specified rights transferred to him by Sigismund was that of redeeming all existing mortgages, some of which had run for over a century, and it was most necessary to take account of what the actual values might be after all obligations were liquidated. It was for this purpose that two of his Burgundian financiers, the above-mentioned Poinsot and Pellet, proceeded to make an investigation, continued by another commission in 1473. There had, indeed, been an earlier commission, but this had done little more than take formal possession in the name of Charles of Burgundy. The summary of the reports of these commissions revealed a sorry state of affairs.

The itemized list of the ceded territories as listed in the treaty was far from telling the extent of poverty really acquired. In the first place, the Austrian seigniories were scattered here and there in the midst of land ruled by others,— bishops, abbots, cities, or the count palatine. Then the variety in the extent and nature of Austrian title, where it did exist, was extraordinary. Nearly every possible combination of dismembered prerogative and actual tenure had resulted from the long series of complicated mortgages and sales. In some localities a toll or a quit-rent was the sole item that had been mortgaged, and again a toll or a prerogative was the only remnant of ownership remaining to the ostensible overlord, while all his nominal property or transferable birthright privileges were lodged in various hands on diverse tenures. Certain monopolies, regal in nature, such as jurisdiction of passports and control of the highways, had not been alienated any more than the suzerainty. This last comprised the right to confer fiefs, that of requisition of military service, and *le droit de forteresse jurable et rendable.*

The compact between Charles and Sigismund, however, differed from all these previous minor covenants, not only in degree but in kind, for the Duke of Burgundy entered into the *sovereign* as well as the mangled, maimed, and curtailed tax-imposing, law-giving, proprietary rights of the hereditary overlord. As a result, Charles, a French peer, came as Landgrave into the circle of the Empire. But that was not for him really a new position. He was already under feudal obligations to the Emperor for part of Burgundy and for other fiefs, although the duty sat lightly upon him.

No real gain came to Charles from the Treaty of St. Omer. The Austrian dukes had not been popular in Alsace, but their poverty had prevented them from being hard masters even where they retained the right to exert any local authority at all. But the Burgundian was determined to be ruler *de facto*. Peter de Hagenbach, his governor, was instructed to bring order out of chaos, and in his efforts to fulfil his instructions he made himself the worst hated *Landvogt* in the memory of Alsatians. His resolve to reduce the free city of Mulhouse to the status of the mortgaged lands was especially resented, and he was finally executed according to the sentence of an angry tribunal, which hardly had more than a shadow of legality in its composition. Moreover tradition and legend has heaped obloquy upon the man until he is represented as a very devil, hardly equalled by Gessler of Swiss fame.

Before the death of Charles at Nancy in 1477, Sigismund had drawn back the Alsace estates to the Habsburgs. His friends rallied around him when they saw what Charles was about. Money was found for the Archduke, who was enabled to offer his creditor full redemption, with the required payment in one sum. Charles had refused to accept this and, as far as appears clearly, no money ever did return to the Burgundian treasury. For the time, however, at any rate, the Sundgau and the county of Ferrette were again Austrian, with the tangle of debts and mortgages probably still unravelled.[13]

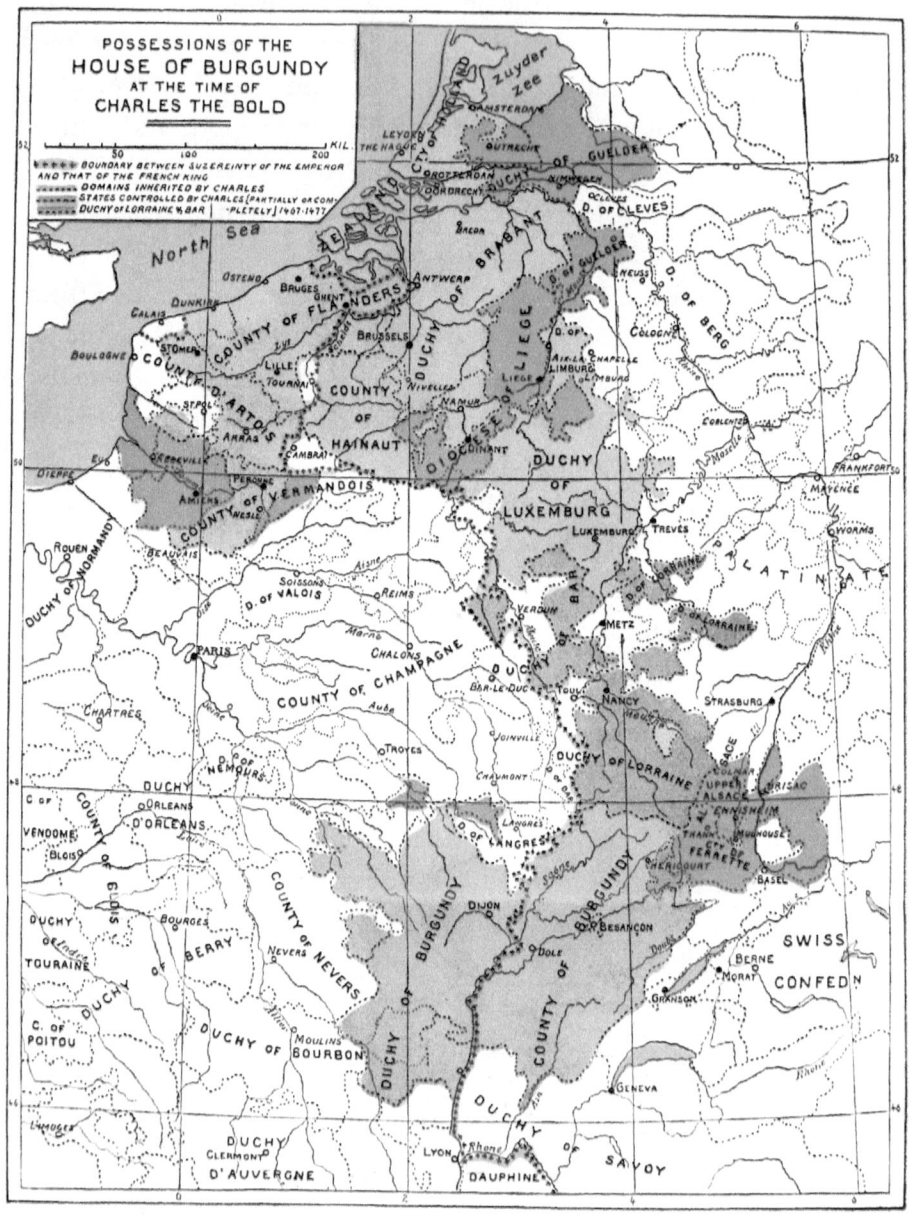

MAP NO. 4

---

[13] The end of this incident belongs to the story of Lorraine. See Map IV.

IV.

THE PEOPLE OF ALSACE IN THE FIFTEENTH CENTURY AND AFTER

WHILE it is comparatively easy to get visions of Alsace and her people in a state of unrest and of opposition to some distasteful authority, it is rather difficult to obtain an insight into her more peaceful existence. But there are sufficient indications to show that there was time between troublous episodes for busy and profitable industry, and that, moreover, there was a tendency to remember but lightly some of their inflictions. Rhymes and popular jingles record many Alsatian events. For instance there was a wine cask, long preserved in the cellar of the Strasburg Hospital, dating from the time of the Burgundian occupation, bearing an inscription which may be translated as follows:

1472

Dear Friend, hereon I let you know
That a good wine lies here below,
Which grew, I'd only say to you,
In fourteen hundred and seventy-two.
While the Burgundians made war
I entered in this building's door.

Again a few years later:

1505

This year the grape crop was so fine
That plenteous was the store of wine.
There was so much that day by day
They had to give the wine away.

The years 1753 and 1762 were also marked by wonderful grape harvests, but at other times the rhyming chronicler had a sadder tale to tell in his rhymes.

> In fifteen hundred and thirty-nine
> The barrels did exceed the wine.[14]

Good average years there were in plenty when the vintage is taken as a matter of course and neither praised nor blamed.

The Peasant War of 1525 is thus grimly recorded on a chapel erected at the scene of defeat of the poor rebels, who met their death in a futile endeavour to improve their condition as labourers in the vineyards:

> Is this not a sorry doom,
> Thirteen thousand in one tomb?

So they run on, these rhyming comments. Undoubtedly they pleased the people and that is why Brandt's *Ship of Fools* (1494), with its daring "poetical" attacks on all the vices current in the world, paved the way to popular participation in the great Protestant Revolt of the sixteenth century. Brandt was a Strasburger; he knew how to appeal to Alsatians and he found an audience far afield. Very probably the striking cartoons helped explain the lines and secured a wider circulation for the book. They told their own story. The text was translated into Latin literally and in two imitations, into Dutch three times, into French once, and into English twice. Alexander Barclay was very humble in his hopes that his "presumptuous audacite" would be pardoned when his own English version was issued (1509). There is no doubt that this "best seller" of the very beginning of the sixteenth century came to be a powerful factor in the great conflict that followed shortly. It was special pleading in behalf of the popular side, the cause of the lay folk as against those in office, for those who had begun to read what the printing-presses were just beginning to put within reach of the masses. Pandora's box had been opened and no human power could again close it.

As the sixteenth century progressed, Alsace like the rest of the Rhineland felt the shocks of the Peasant awakening and of the Protestant risings.

In Strasburg, there was a measure of peaceful evolution in civic jurisdiction over individual consciences. Perhaps the burghers had been gradually prepared for this by Sebastian Brandt's laugh,—one of the Strasburg canons

---

[14] *Alsatia*, Jahrbuch. Ed. August Stöber, p. 87.

was named "The Fool" in honour of the book,—by Martin Bucer's wise preaching, by Jacob Sturm, who displayed sagacity in the part he played in municipal administration and in negotiations with the Imperial Diet. Erasmus, then a neighbour at Basel, expressed his admiration for the way in which the mass was abolished at Strasburg. In spite of Imperial remonstrances, the question was decided in a Council meeting of February 20, 1529, by the franchises of the *échevins—schoeffen* or sheriffs as the title is inaccurately rendered in English. Twenty-one out of the three hundred members of this ultimate power of the civic republic failed to appear. One hundred and eighty-four votes were cast for the immediate abolition of the ancient rite; ninety-four for a postponement of the question until after the decision of the Imperial Diet; one single voice was lifted in behalf of its retention, and the matter was settled.

At the same time, the city was liberal towards those who accepted different creeds of the new faith, and it afforded refuge to many fugitives from persecution elsewhere. Even the Anabaptists were protected in Strasburg.

But if the city of Strasburg passed through the religious crisis smoothly, it was not so with Habsburg Alsace. There occurred considerable persecution and much misery. The theologic affiliations of different parts of the region were curiously different, too, some cities being affected by Swiss, others by Palatine ideas, while others submitted easily to reactionary influence.

The Reformation in Alsace has been compared to a glowing firebrand, passing along and kindling a conflagration[15] wherever there was not a hand ready to extinguish the flames instantly—a comparison suggestive of the persistently fractional and sectional character of Alsace.

There was every reason why these petty yet bitter disputes, added as they were to the incessant feudal broils and to the recurrent efforts of the peasants to better their condition, should have desolated Alsatian territory.[16] But the testimony of one visitor to the land just after these disturbances shows that it continued to make a favourable impression upon the traveller. Sebastian Münster,[17] who saw it about 1540, expatiates on its fertility, declaring that no other Rhineland can compare with it. This was owing especially to the many

---

[15] Lorenz and Scherer, p. 208.
[16] *Alsatia*, i., p. 5.
[17] *Kosmographie*.

little streams that flow down from the Vosges Mountains to the Ill and to the Rhine. This fertility enabled the inhabitants to export their surplus of wine and corn. Excellent pastureland and silver mines were also at the disposal of the people to make them find their lot better than that of other men. Perhaps this richness is the reason why he finds a disinclination to save the products of industry, for Münster adds that a lean year brings great distress, though all are willing to help each other. The observer finds the population very mixed, ethnographically, with immigration still active from both the Germanic and French quarters; he remarks that there is a continual drift of newcomers from Swabia, Bavaria, Burgundy, and Lorraine, everyone who can help in the harvest being welcomed gladly.

V.

THE THIRTY YEARS' WAR AND THE PEACE OF WESTPHALIA

THE century after Münster thus testified to Alsatia's charm brought the bitterest of all her hard experiences. Havoc worse than any inflicted by local disturbances was wrought to city and country by the prolonged hostilities of the Thirty Years' War (1618–1648). Alsace was not only dragged into its complications but was forced again and again, much to her own detriment, to serve as a battlefield. That confused period of international warfare, begun under the pretext of upholding territorial religion, according to the doctrine that the land must follow the creed of its ruler—*cujus regio, ejus religio*,—proceeded under fresh impulses of divers kinds. A weak association of Protestant princes was banded against a Catholic League and feeble emperor. In course of time, stronger powers entered into the fray, Gustavus Adolphus of Sweden being hailed by Protestant Germany as a deliverer. After his death in 1634, all unity of Catholics or Protestants became obscured and weakened, and for the succeeding fourteen years, Germany at large was simply the battleground of French, Spanish, Austrian, and Swedish hordes, striving for personal ends, but all alike skilled in the science of plunder as learned in the school of Mansfeld and Wallenstein. Every country they touched in Europe was reduced to a state of misery that no historian has been able to describe, save by detailing the horrors of one or more villages among the thousands ruined. The motives of combatants, possibly clear at the beginning, became mixed and confused or even shifted from side to side. At times, the old chimera of the "Middle Kingdom" loomed up to make France fearful of Spain in her conquests along the eastern boundary of France. Everyone distrusted everyone else. Anne of Austria, Richelieu, Tilly, Condé, Wallenstein, Louis XIII., were among those involved in the earlier stages of the conflict, Mazarin and Louis XIV. at the end and in the later seventeenth-century wars that followed on the close of the first general peace. Richelieu pursued a steady policy of reducing places which might aid to extend the French frontier and it was partly as a result of this policy that the border landgraviates of the Vosges as well as Lorraine were, continuously, scenes of hostilities.[18] Alsace itself, overrun and harassed by Swedes, Austrians, and French,—one Alsatian city was within a brief period taken and retaken ten times,—was actually slipped under French control by Bernard of Saxe-Weimar, the man who, after the death of Gustavus Adolphus, took command at Lützen, a German and a Protestant, so strange were the friendships made through mixed motives of enmity towards other foes. This soldier of fortune, one of the many picturesque figures of the cosmopolitan group of striking personalities, found it expedient, in behalf of the Protestant cause and his own interests, to accept the aid of Catholic France. The little independent army he had mustered had to be supported and Bernard's patrimony as a seventh son was inadequate to the burden. His own fortune was to be carved out, too, and the Saxon knight errant dreamed of founding a line of Alsatian dukes. Had he outlived Richelieu, this ambition might have been realized. At his death, his troops had practical control of both Upper and Lower Alsace. Bernard was only thirty-five and had every prospect of a long life when a fever carried him off, unexpectedly, in 1639. The troops were, thus, left suddenly without a commander. Richelieu saw his opportunity, assumed their maintenance, and secured the conquests of his late ally. The soldiers accepted the assurance that Bernard, whom they had honoured as a prince, was really nothing more than their commanding officer and that they belonged less to him than to the French king from whom he and they alike had drawn pay. The ever bi-lingual frontier nature of Alsace is again emphasized in the stipulation that the garrisons should consist half of German, half of French troops, and the lingering theological character of the war and the fact that France was helping the German Protestants, by the pledge that there should be no interference with the free exercise of the Protestant religion either in the conquered places or in the army. These "Bernardine" troops remained in Alsace as headquarters for many years, always refusing to fight outside Germany or for any cause except that of German and Protestant liberty. A secret treaty had been signed in Paris (October 27, 1635) between soldier and statesman providing that the landgraviate of Alsace, together with all the rights therein of the House of Austria, should be secured to the former. Before his death, Bernard made a

---

[18] See Reuss, *L'Alsace au XVIIe siècle*, i., p. 125.

will nominating one Hans Ludwig Erlach of Berne his successor as commander, and one of his brothers as heir to his property, or rather to his claims. Among other articles one provided for the return of Alsatian territories to Imperial supremacy at the close of the war. Erlach did, indeed, succeed Bernard as commander, but under circumstances that threw a shadow on his reputation, while little further attention was paid to Bernard's bequests.

During the years of more or less desultory warfare that followed between the initiation of peace negotiations in 1642 and their final consummation in the Peace of Westphalia,[19] Alsace was held in the interests of the French. At first indeed, the garrison was bi-national and the exercise of the Protestant religion was scrupulously permitted. But after a little time such consideration was lost sight of. When the diplomatic settlement came, the House of Habsburg was willing to accept the alienation of its hereditary right in the Vosges tract. There was no one person to protest.

Since the abdication of Charles V., the Empire had lost its prestige. The Ferdinands—II. and III.—of the Thirty Years' War were not great personage, or able to hold their own against the French statesmen growing more definitely aggressive in their plans for France. The Empire became *de facto* a mere federation, with loose structure at that. It had no common treasury, no efficient tribunals; its states were of different creeds, were governed according to different forms, and were administered judicially and financially without any regard to each other. The fundamental debility was the natural result of the fact that half the sovereigns remained *without* the authority of Rome. For if the Roman Empire were regarded as the shadow of the Popedom, it was designed to rule over men's bodies as the Pontiff ruled over their souls, and the enfeebling of the one seriously affected the other. The documents that were accepted as the conclusion of the Thirty Years' War—the Treaties of Westphalia—phrased, specified, and crystallized an existant condition. The signatories to the group of compacts comprised in that Peace recognized, formally, a large number of Lutherans and Calvinists as free from the jurisdiction of Pope or Catholic prelate. The last nominal link that bound Germany *as a whole* to Rome was snapped.

---

[19] From the very beginning of the war there had been many attempts to compose differences and a certain number of documents had been interchanged between various parties—and disregarded, as a rule.

Lord Bryce ranks this Peace of Westphalia[20] as marking an era in the history of the Holy Roman Empire as clearly defined as did the coronation of Otto the Great or the death of Frederick II. The "Empire" left was really no Empire at all, but an association of German states,—a fact emphasized by the number of military frontiers that obtained. In the nineteenth century, before 1866, there were still a confusing array of political units, possessing "rights" or privileges for money-coining, toll-collecting, title-conferring, etc., but two centuries earlier there were *three hundred and forty-three* such units, originated or confirmed when the Peace of Westphalia emancipated the petty princes from Imperial control and left them masters each in his diminutive territory. Had Bernard of Saxe-Weimar lived to realize his vision of the two Alsace districts combined within the ring fence of one neat little duchy re-attached to the Imperial domain at the close of the war, this too would very possibly have been included in the solar system of the Empire. But Bernard died in Alsace, as Charles of Burgundy died in Lorraine. Their dreams, the lesser and the greater ambition together, vanished, while Richelieu's declared desire "To give to Gaul the frontiers which Nature had designed for it, to secure to the Gauls a Gallic king, to identify Gaul with France, and wherever the ancient Gaul was there to establish the new," was realized, at least in part, by his successors.

The contracting powers thus definitely consented that Alsace should recede within the limits of the ancient Gaul discovered by the Romans, "divided into three parts." The dividing line between Celtic and Germanic territories in that part of the Rhine Valley was to be, and finally was, no longer the Vosges Mountains but the river itself, the river which Cæsar forced Ariovistus *rex Germanorum* to recross and which the migrating Swabians concluded not to attempt at that time.

Thus by another whim of Fate—had the Lady of Destiny any method in her madness?—Alsace was not comprised within the federation, classed by Lord Bryce as the first distinctively German Empire, any more than it was with the Germanic realm created at Verdun, which celebrated its millennial birthday in 1843.

---

[20] *Holy Roman Empire*, chap. xix.

There is no ambiguity in Article 75[21] of the Treaty of Münster—one contribution towards the Peace of Westphalia:

> The Emperor, in his own behalf and in that of the most serene House of Austria, cedes the rights, properties, domains, possessions, and jurisdictions which hitherto belonged to him, to the Empire, and to the House of Austria, in the city of Breisach, the landgraviates of Upper and Lower Alsace, the Sundgau, the prefecture general of the ten imperial cities situated in Alsace . . . and all the countries and other rights of whatever nature, which are comprised within this prefecture,—by transferring all and each to the very Christian King and to the realm of France.

The succeeding article declares that the cession is made for all time "without any reservation, with plenary jurisdiction and superiority and sovereignty for ever . . . so that no emperor and no prince of the House of Austria can or *ought* ever at any time to make pretensions to or usurp any right and puissance over the said lands," and Article 79[22] adds that the Emperor, the Empire, and the Archduke Ferdinand Charles shall discharge all officials in the ceded territory from their oaths of fealty towards themselves.

These phrases seemed to show an intention of releasing the whole tract to which the name "Alsace" had been applied. Mazarin spoke of France having obtained *"une grande province."* Very possibly even he did not realize the complexity of the tenure of suzerainty and of property rights in the two *gauen*.

But, as a matter of fact, the treaty stipulations in its regard did not end here. Article 89[23] adds a reservation in respect to all *États* holding direct from the Emperor. Imperial cities, seigniories, nobles of Lower Alsace, monasteries, etc., were to be left in full enjoyment of their *immediatété* towards the Holy Roman Empire and it was expressly stated that the King was, in each and every case, to refrain from claiming any royal supremacy. He was to rest content with the rights and privileges that had belonged to the Archduke and had been ceded "to the crown of France by this Treaty of Peace."

---

[21] The numbering of the articles follows Vast, *Les grands traités du regne de Louis XIV.*, p. 38. They are given differently by other editors.

[22] Vast, p. 40.

[23] Vast, p. 44.

Here was palpable contradiction,—a contradiction again weakened by the words "so however, that by the present declaration, it be not understood that there should be any prejudice to the sovereign rights previously accorded."

How could the Emperor hold on to his supremacy if said sovereign rights had been previously alienated and if the alienation were not to be prejudiced?

Neither at that time nor ever afterwards was any one able to solve the knotty problem—so it was cut, as hard knots have been out before. As far back as 1646, the points concerning the degree of sovereignty acquired by France in the peace preliminaries had been hotly discussed. Mazarin had held out for the terms that seemed to imply "the cession of a great province, mentioned by him as achieved." Possibly the reservations were inserted to save the pride of the Imperial envoys. Possibly no one planned deliberate obscurity. In treaties and wills phrases sometimes slip in between several revisions and no one reviser really intended malice aforethought or designedly made fresh phrases contradictory to the old. The crucial question remained: did the French King succeed simply to the powers exercised by the Archduke and become the Emperor's vassal as the Habsburger had been, or were not only the Archduke's possessions and dignities, the landgraviate and the simple prefecture of Haguenau, but the ten cities as well transferred to him and withdrawn from the Empire for ever? As a matter of fact, no one seems at first to have considered a complete severance from the Empire. There was some disposition to assume that the French King would follow the landgrave and would accordingly be entitled to a seat at the Imperial Diet and a voice in affairs Imperial and German. In the seventeenth century this was not at all an impossible state of political affairs. The complete withdrawal of each nationality into itself is really a modern condition. Much territory held as an Imperial fief was far from German soil and the overlord bore other and more important titles. Witness the little principality of Orange lying on the Rhine north of Avignon. In 1648, that still had no political relation to the kings of France. It was an Imperial fief until 1714, for more than half a century after the Peace of Westphalia. But neither the Emperor nor the princes of the Empire really desired the presence of a French king at the Diet in any capacity, and on the part of Mazarin there was some reluctance to have him accredited there as a simple landgrave, even though other advantages might accrue.

In 1848, Alsace celebrated the two hundredth anniversary of her annexation to France. But that was claiming for the whole what only belonged to a part. There is no doubt that immediately after the Peace, Mazarin made no attempt to claim more than very partial and fragmentary French sovereignty in Alsace. An indemnity of three million livres was provided for the Archduke Charles Ferdinand as compensation for his lost landgraviate and prefecture. The French monarch stepped into his vacated shoes. Later, as Louis XIV. began to act in his own behalf, came the extension of further control over Alsace, appropriated with more or less disregard of other vested rights, civic, territorial, or imperial, but never did the king present himself as a member of the Imperial Circle by virtue of his new possession, any more than the various honorary colonels of European regiments have put forth their claims to be recognized in this year 1914 in the dignities once so pleasantly conferred upon them.

But while the treaty certainly did not bestow Alsace upon the French King, it did give him a point of departure whence he could proceed to extend his sovereignty. At the beginning, however, there was certainly no question of a total separation between Alsace and Germany.[24] The former was considered in the *douane* regulation as *un pays d'étranger effective*, closed on the French and opened on the German side. A letter from Louis XIV., then thirteen years old (1651), to the magistrate and senate of Haguenau, shows an intention to make the "protection," legally his, as definite as possible:

> Very dear and good friends, by the treaty of the Peace of the Empire happily concluded, the land graviate of Alsace was ceded to us together with the protection of the ten imperial cities. We have appointed to the government of the said country and of the bailiwick of Haguenau our dear and beloved cousin Henri de Lorraine, Count d'Harcourt, grand knight of France, as a person most capable of worthily fulfilling the function. We wished to inform you by this letter so that you would not make any difficulty about recognizing him in this quality and that you will accord to him the same honour and deference that you did to the Archduke of Austria, when he commanded in Alsace under the authority of the Emperor; and we promise that you shall have

---

[24] M. Lavisse lays stress upon this point, vol. vii., p. 19.

good relations with our said cousin, whom we have commanded to maintain you in your ancient privileges and immunities.[25]

The King's good friends at Haguenau were not at all inclined to accept "his dear cousin" so readily. The Austrian *landvogt* had let them go pretty easily along their own way, and they were afraid that the new régime was not to be equally *laisser-faire*. Moreover the tone of the French King's letter seemed to imply that he, or his minister on the minor's behalf, was speaking more like an imperial overlord than a simple prefect.

Protests, arguments, and armed interference followed before the Alsatian towns finally acquiesced and bowed to French sovereignty. Mulhouse had been recognized by the Peace of Westphalia as independent and free to join the Swiss League—now without the Empire—and Strasburg was on its own basis. They were not exposed to the same pretensions as the towns of the Decapole, as they were called. But these last, small as some of them were, had rejoiced in their freedom to manage their own affairs with direct dependence upon the Emperor. All had votes in the Diets, maintained military contingents, and enjoyed the privilege of appeal to the supreme tribunal of the Empire. This substantial independence they were most unwilling to lose. Nor was it considered, even in France, that they had lost it, for they continued to send representatives to the Diet, long after Louis XIV. made good his demands.

It soon became plain that Louis XIV. had a greater strength in his own behalf than either Richelieu or Mazarin had possessed for France or for him. The Westphalian treaties brought no peace to Europe. The Fronde followed, and after it came other wars that were certainly no child's play, each followed by a Peace that did not mean tranquillity. Yet each successive diplomatic adjustment at the close of each series of hostilities settled France a little more securely in the coveted possession of Alsace. In the Treaty of the Pyrenees (1659) the King of Spain, as member of the House of Habsburg, ratified the cession of family rights in the Sundgau, although, apparently, the stipulated indemnity had never been paid on the plea that the Habsburgs had failed to fulfil other obligations. Louis XIV. felt encouraged to push his pretensions further. In 1661, his newly appointed governor of the ten cities, the Duke de

---

[25] September 17, 1651. Legrelle, *Louis XIV. et Strasbourg*, p. 738.

Mazarin, attempted to exact a more defined oath of fidelity and obedience to the King, as to their sovereign lord. It was firmly refused, and a formula *plus anodyne* was substituted.

The differences between Louis XIV. and the Empire again came to open war, and brought a period of fresh distress to Alsace. French troops occupied cities and province and finally the King's victories enabled him to confirm a situation *de facto* which had dated from August, 1673. When the next "Peace" was discussed at Nimeguen, Louis XIV. was in a position to dictate terms. The status of the ten cities was one of the burning questions absorbing the Imperial envoys. They came primed to reassert their "immediacy" in the Empire. But the point of possession was against them. Only Wissenburg and Landau held Imperial garrisons, while the remaining eight were actually in French hands. In the first proposition put forth by the French plenipotentiaries the ten cities were not mentioned at all. All they asked was the re-establishment of the Peace of Westphalia. There were then counter propositions of arbitration—upon the true meaning of that same document—something Louis XIV. might have accepted ten years earlier but which at this date he refused. Discussion was long and heated and French diplomacy won out. On February 5, 1679, the Treaty of Nimeguen was signed by the Imperial and French plenipotentiaries. It was ratified by Louis XIV. February 26th, by the Diet, March 23d, and by the Emperor, the 29th. As far as the ten cities were concerned their situation was unchanged diplomatically. Article 2[26] provided that the Treaty of Münster (Westphalia) should be re-established "in each and every item in its ancient vigour." The plenipotentiaries tried to get around the omission by handing in a list of the places France was to evacuate, which contained the names of eight of the towns—Wissenburg and Landau being omitted naturally. It was of no avail.[27] Colbert de Croissy—then Prefect in Alsace—absolutely declined to consider this proposition and demanded in his turn the evacuation of Wissenburg and Landau. He was told that the war would be renewed if he did not accede to the Emperor's demands—a futile argument in the exhausted state of Imperial resources! When the articles of execution of the treaty were signed on July 17, 1679, Louis XIV. pledged himself to restore,

---

[26] See Vast, *Traités de Nimégue et Tréve de Ratisbonne*, p. 103.

[27] See Georges Bardot, *Dix villes impériales d'Alsace*, p. 260, Paris, 1899. He and Legrelle seem to be fairer in their treatment of the subject than Sybel, Scherer, or even Voltaire.

in addition to certain specified territories, "all the places not belonging to him either in virtue of the Treaty of Münster or of the Treaty of Nimeguen," while the Emperor agreed to cede Wissenburg and Landau by name.[28] There was a complete failure of the attempt to introduce a clause into the new treaty reinterpreting the ambiguous phrases of the old to the satisfaction of the Emperor and of the ten cities themselves, and to annul the successive measures enacted by Louis XIV. from 1673 on the basis of the interpretation that suited him. The only result of the futile efforts was to furnish further documentary support to French pretensions. As the plenipotentiaries could not get their interpretation accepted, the opposite interpretation was practically legitimated.

From that date on the French King abandoned the rather timid policy he had inaugurated in regard to the ten cities, and henceforth simply relied on the treaty provisions interpreted in the fashion most favourable to his interests. Once again in 1679 the cities were asked to accept the oath they had refused in 1661, and they promised almost without resistance "to be faithful and obedient to the King, our gracious sovereign and sovereign protector, and to recognize M. de Montclar as our grand bailiff."

Colmar alone held out when the oath was offered in September, but finally decided to submit, and the proud little municipalities were brought under French sovereignty, just as had been done thirty years back with the Sundgau and other Habsburg dependencies. A *Conseil d'Alsace*[29] was established to save the good people the "expense and fatigue involved in appealing to the *parlement* at Metz." This was to be a sovereign court. Its first duty was to assert that the "réunion" to France of all the territories was conferred upon Louis XIV. by the Treaty of Münster and confirmed by that of Nimeguen.

---

[28] Bardot, p. 266.
[29] See map.

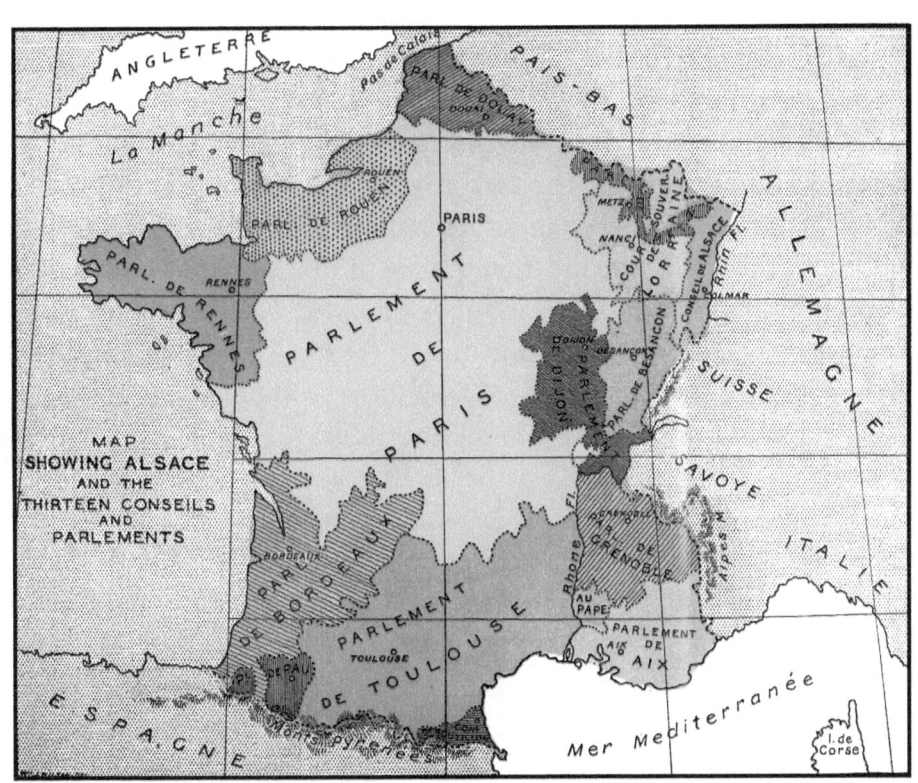

MAP NO. 5

VI.

LOUIS XIV. AND STRASBURG

THERE was a pretence of diplomatic sanction for the so-called "réunions" of the little cities, but the fashion in which Strasburg was brought under the French flag can hardly be described by any euphemistic terms. Her annexation terminated the long career of a civic unit as a respected and dignified member of the Holy Roman Empire. From all general provisions touching Alsatian cities Strasburg had invariably been excepted, but the ambitious French monarch felt that it was a "military necessity" to avoid having a little free-handed republic, pretending to regard the Emperor as her overlord, but really independent, imbedded in his realm. His attack on her when at peace with the Empire cannot be defended. French authorities have no hesitation in censuring the action in severe terms. The only argument that could be urged is that no country is without possessions whose seizure has been open to criticism, even when diplomatically approved later. And that is a poor enough argument, whether for the seventeenth century or the twentieth.

Strasburg was nothing more than a tiny city state at the mercy of a nation waxing in centralized power. The weakened Empire took little cognizance of her or her plight.[30] Louis XIV. the determined, Louvois the astute statesman, Montclar the efficient general, Vauban the skilled engineer, were a powerful combination for one lone town. Moreover, it happened that when Louvois demanded submission to the King in September, 1681, it was shortly after the magistrates had dismissed the force of Swiss mercenaries that had been employed by them as a military force. This was in order to cut down expenses. Besides that, the majority of the burghers able to fight in their own defence were at the Frankfort Fair. Appeal to the Emperor had been in vain. The republic had often had friction with her sovereign chief, from disagreements as to what each might rightfully demand from the other, and very probably

---

[30] I find reference to a secret article in the Treaty of Nimeguen relating to Strasburg, but I have not seen it.

suggestions had been made to the burgomasters that the French monarch might, on the whole, prove a more convenient friend than the Emperor. At any rate, a letter[31] was despatched to Leopold I. informing him that they had been notified by M. de Montclar that the sovereign chamber of Breisach had adjudged to the King the sovereignty of "all Alsace, of which our city is member," and that "in virtue of such decree, he asked us to recognize His said Majesty for our sovereign seigneur and receive his garrison." If they refrained from resisting this demand, by force of arms, they had been assured that all their ancient rights should be respected. "As we feel too feeble to oppose a puissance so grand and terrible as that of the most Christian King and we see no hope of assistance, we have no other resource but to submit to the will of God and to accept the conditions prescribed by His Most Christian Majesty."

The burgomasters were hurried on to a speedy capitulation. Louvois declared that he must have an answer at break of day. The good servants of the people asked a postponement to noon, "for our Democratic State does not permit a decision of affairs of importance without participation of the entire bourgeoisie, in whom we will endeavour to instil the same sentiments that we ourselves feel—that is to report to Your Excellency an answer which would be agreeable to him."[32]

Louvois objected to any delay, the consent of the "bourgeoisie" was obtained in some manner, and at four o'clock of September 30th, the French troops marched into Strasburg through open gates and not a drop of blood was shed!

The articles of capitulation apparently assured the citizens about the same *modus vivendi* they had always enjoyed. Louvois changed three points in the draft submitted.[33] While he confirmed protection to Protestantism, he insisted on appropriating the Cathedral for Catholic rites, though he reserved to the magistracy the privilege of ringing the bells on occasions of public fêtes. All suits involving more than one thousand livres were removed from civic courts to the jurisdiction of the Council of Alsace. The existing store of ammunition was to be delivered to the French immediately. At the same time, he offered some other concessions voluntarily.

---

[31] Legrelle, p. 554.
[32] Legrelle, p. 560.
[33] *Ibid.*, p. 561.

The terms were probably better reading than they were as a rule for the daily existence of submissive citizens obliged to live under French sovereignty.

> Multis annis jam peractis
> Nulla fides est in pactis;
> Mel in ore, verba lactis,
> Fel in corde, fraus in factis,

were words as true of the pledges made to Strasburg at her capitulation as of other scraps of white paper fair with solemn promises. Honey certainly was not spared by French authorities. For instance, nominally the Revocation of the Edict of Nantes was not valid for Strasburg. But that did not mean that Protestantism continued to be flourishing there. A steady flow of Catholic influence made itself felt in many ways, covert and overt alike.

Louis XIV. felt that the good will of the city was worth wooing. To counteract the sinister effect of his troops marching in as conquerors, he hastened to pay a friendly visit. He lost no time in announcing formally to his Court that he was about to take a little journey in order to receive "the oath of fealty which the Treaty of Nimeguen empowered him to receive from Strasburg." It was a splendid cavalcade that travelled across the country to Alsace. The Queen avoided the high passes of the Vosges and went by way of St. Dié, while the King rode over the mountain barrier that had separated his newly acquired lands from France. Louvois was on hand at St. Dié to welcome the Queen and to receive her congratulations for his great achievement accomplished without bloodshed. On October 23d, the stately entry of the Grand Monarch into the old town was made, the cortège gay with banners and with the ladies' dresses, too brilliant to look like what it really was,—the funeral procession of one of the oldest city republics in Europe.

Here is a letter despatched to Strasburg the week before this pompous seal was set on the "annexation." It was written by M. Jalon to M. Güntzer from Metz on October 11, 1681:[34]

> Monsieur, I do not doubt that the change that has occurred in your Republic touches you greatly and that the beginnings will seem rude and

---

[34] See Legrelle, *Louis XIV. et Strasbourg*, p. 798. From "Correspondance politique adressée eu Magistrat de Strasbourg par ses agents à Metz."

difficult to endure, but wise people such as you are in your Republic are accustomed to submit patiently to the will of Divine Providence wisely directing all things and making them redound to His glory and our salvation. The change has greatly astonished and touched us at the same time more than I can tell you, but I do not dare to express all my sentiments, knowing that Mgr. de Louvois might arrest your couriers and that this letter might be seen; I assure you, however, that due consideration will show that this misfortune has its consolation. For you have obtained by the capitulation all that you could reasonably expect, there being little appearance that your cathedral, your cannon, and your arms would be secured to you. You might have had more to fear if your cannon and arms had been left to you, for in that case your actions would have been more rigidly and scrupulously watched, and at the least suspicion, some screw might have been turned upon you to reduce you to a state worse than that you now endure. As for me I could wish we were in the same condition. We should think ourselves happy if we were, but we must each be content with what God wills, provided we can find therein a quiet conscience. I should have been glad to hear from you the details of what has happened. But I know you have had too much on hand, and that surprise and dismay prevented your thinking of sending news to your friends. But now that the storm is quieting, and the fury abated, you might do so. I am surprised that the last courier arriving here from Strasburg brought no news from you. I don't think, though, they will prevent our friendly relations, and deny us the intercourse by letter that we cannot have face to face, and I await your opinion about it. Still I will tell you that it is said here that you have been deputed to go to His Majesty to assure him of your submission and fidelity to his service. In this I think you have acted wisely and prudently to try and gain the affection of the great King which may in future be most useful to you. He is a gracious and obliging prince, so that I have no doubt of your finding him favourable to you. It is thought here that he has just left Vitry with the Queen and the Court to go into Alsace....

The next diplomatic settlement of international affairs took place at Ryswick sixteen years after Strasburg's surrender. The various treaties comprised within this "Peace" stipulated more renunciations by Louis XIV. than accessions to his realm. But the article securing *Urbs Argentinensis*—the ancient Roman name lived on in all documents—to the French crown was confused by no ambiguity of terms. Strasburg was to be considered as incorporated to it for ever—"in perpetuum ad Regem Christianissimum ejus que successores pertineat et Coronæ Galliæ incorporata intelligatur."[35]

"Thanks to the preciseness of this stipulation, henceforth Strasburg, in law as in fact, belonged to France,"[36] says M. Legrelle, adding that it was no gratuitous surrender on the Emperor's part. Article 18 ceded Kehl,—19, Freiburg,—and 20, Breisach, as compensation for the city lost to Imperial sovereignty.[37]

On the whole, it may be said that the Emperor's loss was a shadowy one. The loss was Strasburg's own. She deliberately renounced her freedom for fear of a worse fate if she resisted. Her incorporation into France was much like what Belgium's might be. A piece of territory was not stolen from one monarch to the advantage of another. Rather was a small business incorporated in a large one.

The seal of diplomatic acceptance of the "annexation" was not sufficiently satisfactory to still all protests against the act of Louis XIV. in Strasburg and elsewhere in Germany. One Schrag published two vehement pamphlets on the subject, *Libertas Argentoratensium stylo Rysvicenci non expuncta*, 1707, and *Nullitas iniquitasque reunionis Alsaticæ*, 1708. Very possibly had the transfer of territory and free city together been effected at one decisive blow, the dissatisfaction would have been allayed more speedily. But the severance of Alsace from the Empire was very gradual and there was space for murmurs between the steps.

In 1648, France acquired from the House of Habsburg, personally, 284 communities with 226,900 inhabitants; in 1679, from the Empire, 313 communities with 402,600 inhabitants. Later 202 communities were added.[38] But even after the Peace of Ryswick about fifty communities in Alsace remained under German sovereignty, from one title or another. The confused holdings found by the Burgundian were slow in losing their complexity. It took the great convulsion of the French Revolution to do it. When the Constituent Assembly had swept away for good and all the last lingering traces

---

[35] Vast, *Traités de Turin et de Ryswick*, p. 237.

[36] *Ibid.*

[37] "Grace à la netteté de cette stipulation, désormais Strasbourg, en droit comme en fait, appartenait bien à la France." Legrelle, p. 668.

[38] These figures are taken from Sybel, *Deutschland's Rechte auf Elsass und Lothringen*.

of feudalism in the French domain, the question arose, "Did France have the right to deprive the German proprietors in Alsace of those feudal privileges which had been more or less guaranteed at the Peace of Westphalia and confirmed by subsequent treaties?" In February, 1790, certain princes, knightly orders, and knights of the Holy Roman Empire who held land in Alsace, sent a protest to the French government. The protest was referred to the Feudal Committee of the Constituent Assembly. The Committee, under the influence of Merlin of Douai, in October, 1790, brought its report before the Assembly. They asserted that the union of France and Alsace rested on the unanimous decision of the Alsatians; that ancient treaties and the stipulations of their former rulers could no longer bind a free people. Mirabeau thought such a declaration would bring war. He persuaded the Assembly to pass a resolution to uphold the sovereignty of France in Alsace, but at the same time to ask the King that an indemnity should be paid to the princes of the Empire in compensation for their losses. This resolution only postponed the question for the majority of the princes declined any monetary compensation and took their case to the Imperial Diet.[39]

Not long after this incident Louis XVI. lost his significance, later so did the Empire. Feudalism vanished from Alsace, and other points of national sovereignty were settled by the Treaty of Basel, signed by France and Prussia, April 5, 1795. This gave France a free hand on the left bank of the Rhine, in return for pledges to respect a line of demarcation which virtually placed northern Germany under Prussian control.

---

[39] *Cambridge Modern History*, vol. viii, p. 398.

VII.

ALSACE AFTER ANNEXATION TO FRANCE

THUS it was not until the French Revolution with its holocaust of feudal relics of a dead past that Alsace became entirely and completely French. It was indeed only in the latter half of the eighteenth century that she had time to give serious thought to her nationality. The Peace of Ryswick had brought just as much tranquillity to Europe as the rest of the great documentary adjustments had done. Wars under various names continued to hold the centre of the scene in Europe one after the other, and no border land was unscathed by their ravages, although Alsace never again suffered as severely as in the Thirty Years' War.[40]

But even before the scars of that calamity were really healed her visitors had words of praise for her charms. There are several "impressions" of travellers accessible to our eyes. One Claude Joly, sent to Alsace on a military mission, is very enthusiastic about the land, and so is Jean Koenig, a Jesuit from Freiburg, three years later (1677). The latter declares that Ceres and Pomona decorate the plains, Bacchus smiles down from the hillsides, while the very rocks are not sterile as in other lands, but possess rich veins of silver. A certain geographer greatly enjoys the exquisite perfumes wafted by the breeze from the thousand flower gardens, and still another tourist who sketches *en route*,

---

[40] The population of Alsace in 1695 was rated as follows (from the *Chronique Colmarienne* of Sigismond Billing):

Men (including paupers)	23,343	souls
Nobles	239	"
Clergy, Catholic and Protestant	1,731	"
Women and widows	48,226	"
Young boys	52,915	"
Young girls	51,451	"
Labourers and servants	24,556	"
Heads of families	43,536	"
Total	245,997	souls

also likes Alsace in general but finds the mountains "horrible in their roughness in spite of the radiant fields at their base."[41]

The spurs and peaks which Eduard Grucker finds so "*wunderschön*"[42] were not appreciated in earlier times, except by the castle-builder from utilitarian reasons, but they were rapturously admired by a certain young student from Frankfort, who matriculated at the Alsatian University in 1770. Young Johann Wolfgang Goethe was sent to Strasburg by his father to complete the studies that he had not prosecuted very successfully at Leipzig. How he loved that "beautiful Alsace" and blessed Fate for having cast his lot there for a time![43] It was not only the fairness of the landscape but its prosperity and fruitfulness that gave him profound satisfaction. He loved to think of all the comfortable farmhouses and well-to-do hamlets scattered over the great fertile plain. And then the mountains! To his mind it was a veritable Paradise and he thinks everyone ought to be able to understand how he felt, if they will but consider what Alsace really is. This "Alsatian semi-France" is to him a foreign land and he is alert to all the characteristics of it as though he were a traveller from a much more distant town than Frankfort. When he tries to get data as to the best method of pursuing the study of jurisprudence so as to obtain his degree as quickly as possible, his friend Dr. Salzmann points out to him that Strasburg is much more French than German. They are pre-eminently *practical* instead of "seeking the wide intellectual horizon that is the dream in German Universities."

Then an event happens that diverts the student from his work for the moment. Marie Antoinette passes through the city on her way to be married in Paris, and Strasburg exerts itself to give her a gay welcome. Everything is in festival array as it had been for the visit of Louis XIV. and his Queen ninety years previous. Only in 1681 Strasburg had been the staid mediæval city. In Goethe's time she was in a period of transition. Blondel of Paris had sketched out a plan for beautifying the city and it was to be done, gradually, as new houses were erected on the to-be-widened streets. So the line was crooked, here a new house, back, there an old one, forward. One had to use imagination, says

---

[41] *Mémoires de deux voyages et séjours en Alsace*, 1674–76 and 1681, L. Hermine, Mulhouse, 1886.

[42] *Die Vogesen*, von Eduard Grucker, Leipzig, 1908.

[43] *Wahrheit und Dichtung aus meinen Leben*, chapters ix., x., and xi.

the poet, to realize that a fine city was on its way to completion. Just then it was between form and formlessness.

In spite of the anti-Protestant influence attributed to the French régime, Goethe finds Strasburg markedly Protestant, and then he comments on one phase of life that surprises him: "Allow me, with a sudden change of subject, to mention dancing. Just as the eye is constantly reminded of the Cathedral at every turn in Strasburg, so the ear is of dancing, and not only in Strasburg, but in all Alsace!"

It seems that the elder Goethe had been very particular about teaching his children dancing, but Wolfgang found that home training had its defects and that he was less skilled than the Alsatians. So he takes lessons to bring himself into touch with the (then) modern dances.

But it is the open country that gives Goethe his greatest joy, and he is so in love with it and with the Strasburg fashion of enjoying it by pleasure walking that he considers the advantages of attaching himself to the University as a life career. The reason for his decision adverse to the idea is interesting. Herder and Schöpflin had been among the men who influenced him and he saw prospects of advancement in France if he began his work in Strasburg. He really likes French better than German as a vehicle of expression.

> It had become my own, like a second mother-tongue, without grammar and instruction—by mere intercourse and practice. I now wished to use it with more fluency and had given Strasburg the preference in choosing a second university on that very account. But alas! it was just there that I met with disappointment and took a distaste to the language and to French methods.

In Leipzig, he had been criticized for speaking German too colloquially, but in Alsace he was told that his expressions were archaic, culled as they were from French of all ages, in which he had read very widely, assimilating what he read so that the words came naturally to his lips. He had sturdily defended his choice of German words, gathered from every national source, but cultivated Frenchmen only smiled courteously at his defence of terms which they ostracized from accurate speech. After a time, this exasperated the young German. At first he really desired to be corrected for faults in French conversation. But as he grew interested in the subject-matter of what he was saying the corrections became annoying and broke the thread of all discourse. Then he heard a remark that no foreigner could speak French successfully. "A practised ear can detect a German, Italian, or Englishman under a French mask. One is tolerated but never received into the sanctity of the language."

Schöpflin was allowed to be fairly *au fait* in French but Goethe found, as he probed the question among Frenchmen, a reluctance on their part to admit that any stranger can be really initiate into French feeling. He was told that even Schöpflin indulged in dissertation and dialogue rather than true conversation. "The former was generally recognized as the original and fundamental sin of the Germans, the latter as a cardinal virtue of the French." Further it was claimed that when a foreigner wrote in French, the critics always found so many bones to pick with his manner of expressing himself that his matter was ignored.

What did the embryo poet do? He decided straightway that it would be a vain endeavour to try to attain French standards. The French would overlook his worth because they are slaves to "external conditions."

In short, the poet's fear of French literary arrogance gave him pause and Goethe definitely abandoned the idea of making his career in a French medium. There in the borderland, he decided that he would choose German as the instrument on which he would play his life melody. "Thus on the frontier of France we shed everything French that we had cherished. We found the French way of life too defined and genteel, their poetry cold, their criticism annihilating, their philosophy abstruse, and yet insufficient." Indeed at that crisis, the poet was inclined to turn away from all literary influences, for ever. It was only Shakespeare that brought him to "higher and freer views of life."

He handed in his theses—on what? On a State Church and the importance of all good citizens submitting patiently and decorously to authority! On August 6, 1771, he took his degree and, left Alsace, which had affected him in ways quite contrary to what he had expected. After his revolt from the French side of life there, he sought the German, and found many Alsatians clinging pertinaciously to German ways, in spite of the century of French occupation. Among them there was conversation to his taste and he was free from the criticism that was irksome when he was trying to attain French elegance. In many households he was hospitably received, when he was not making long expeditions to his beloved mountains or shorter tramps to Sesenheim,

Drusenheim, or Zabern on other errands than simple enjoyment of scenery, sincere though the homage was that he gave to the "cheerful, fruitful, joyous land."

In student discussions over political affairs, Goethe acknowledges that the pro-Germans could not say much in praise of their own imperial constitution [the Holy Roman Empire had already been described by Voltaire as neither *Holy*, *Roman*, nor an *Empire*, but it was still in nominal existence], and then adds

> on the other hand, we looked toward the north, we were shone upon by Frederick, the pole star, who was on the eve of making Germany, Europe,— nay the whole world revolve about himself. His preponderance in everything was most strongly manifested when the Prussian exercise and even the Prussian stick was introduced into the French army.

Goethe adds that the curious predilection of the Prussian King for French was annoying to the group of German students but they were glad that the poets and philosophers were treating Frederick as an intruder so that he would be saved to Germany.

In thus describing his own experiences as a student at Strasburg, Goethe unconsciously gives a glimpse into the cross currents of Alsatian life that continued to flow there until the great shock of the French Revolution turned them into one channel that set definitely towards France. It was no unwilling province that was separated from the rest of the Rhineland in 1815. The Prussian power talked of by the Strasburg students gained at the north, but Alsace remained in France by sanction of the Congress of Vienna.

Then came nearly seven decades of national life, the first epoch of national life that Alsace, as a whole, may be said to have had. It was strongly French in sympathy, characterized by certain distinguishing features which were all her own. Certain traits of both nations were preserved, but the sentiment and national pride were French. Throughout the nineteenth century, both languages were spoken by all cultivated people. There had never been any disposition on the part of any French government to suppress the use of German, so it had remained naturally at the service of all who wished it, but French was preferred. The dialect of the common people became almost incomprehensible to Germans. It changed for the worse just as, under French influence, Flemish became a debased form of the language once common to all the Netherlands. The vernacular had no academic standard to keep popular speech at its best. When the new German occupation came in 1871, there was, however, evidence that Germanic speech did not indicate Germanic sentiment. Edmond About went back to his own Saverne,—changed into *Zabern*,—to find the familiar dialect banished from the streets. The peasants would assert stoutly to a Prussian, "*Moi Vranzais, moi pas safoir Allemand,*" with an atrocious accent that betrayed them as "shibboleth" once did another nationality of yore.

Before touching on the events and the sentiments of the last forty years in Alsace, the story of Lorraine must be told in outline.

LORRAINE

THIS term is applied to a region of varying extent, from the great expanse of the original "Lotharii-regnum" to the small area now included in the hyphenated province, Alsace-Lorraine,—*Elsass-Lothringen,*—annexed to the German Empire in 1871. In Merovingian times it was within Austrasia—the Eastern *Reich*. Metz was the capital. The domain allotted to Lothaire, grandson of Charles the Great, by the Treaty of Verdun can be seen by map No. 3, to be literally a "Middle Kingdom" between the realms of his brothers, the Frankish and German kings. As Emperor, his were the two capitals, Rome and Aachen. His lands extended from the North Sea to the centre of Italy, including Switzerland, Lombardy, the Netherlands and Rhinelands. The name, in its Latin form, dates from the reign of the second Lothaire (855). The "regnum" of Lothaire II. was the northern portion of the Middle Kingdom. It covered the regions watered by the Moselle, the Meuse (Maas), and the Schelde, thus comprising the modern Holland, parts of Belgium and Switzerland, etc. The dioceses of Cologne, Trèves, Metz, Toul, Verdun, Liège, Cambrai, Basel, Strasburg, and Besançon were all within its frontiers. The duchy was a portion of this "regnum." The Lorraine of the present German province was a fragment of the old duchy. At the date of its cession (1871) the ancient provincial name was no longer used technically. It had been replaced on the map by the departments of Meuse, Moselle, Meurthe, and Vosges. But in ordinary parlance and in literature, *Lorraine* held its own and its individuality was not forgotten.

I.

RACIAL ELEMENTS

THE story of the vicissitudes through which this segment,—one might say this *heart* of the realm of Lothaire—passed in the course of a thousand years, under its various political affiliations, is a complicated one and can only be touched upon lightly at salient points.

At the moment when Cæsar repulsed Ariovistus and discouraged the Suevi from immediate migration, the region to the north-west of the land of the Sequanians was occupied by three Celtic tribes. *Treviri, Mediomatrici, Leuci*, were the forms given by Cæsar to the names he heard from the natives. *Trèves* is one relic of the nomenclature that prevailed in Gaul. A subordinate tribe name, *Verodunes*, lingers, too, in Verdun. Probably an ancient Celt, returning to his native haunts, would hardly recognize his contribution to modern geographical terminology, any more than an aboriginal American might realize the share of his tribe in certain Indian names when presented in English dress and spelling. The words were simply the best the Romans could do to express the sounds they heard, and they did not cater to Celtic standards. These people were characterized by their early visitors as imaginative, excitable, brave, chivalrous, and ambitious—almost childishly curious and superstitious, very sensitive and thus quick to enter into quarrels and always ready for adventure.

No semblance of civic centres such as existed in western and southern Gaul was to be found among the Treviri and Mediomatrici. They were herders rather than agriculturists, and more interested in horses than cattle. Their dwellings were square or round wooden structures resting on the top of mounds. From the Romans the natives learned the use of stone and brick, and were facile in adapting the materials to their needs. Relics of their handicraft show considerable skill and the germs of civilized development, but at the same time certain primitive traits lingered long among them, especially evident in their religious rites, which sanctified human sacrifice, and in a certain tenacity to their own heritage that made them inhospitable to some phases of higher culture while they accepted others. Menhirs, dolmens, and cromlechs scattered through their thick forests bear witness to a widespread zeal for the early Druidical cult.

After the Roman conquest, the new Celto-Roman world that came into being was permeated with indigenous and imported elements in varying proportions. The Northerners took what they liked from the Roman religion, but they did not forget their own traditions. The old and the new pagan religions became inextricably interwoven. Native gods received Roman names, native rites were adjusted to the new learning. There was, indeed, ample opportunity to acquire things Latin. Intercourse between Celts and Romans was frequent. Metz—Divodurum—is mentioned as early as 67 A. D. By the third century Gaul was a populated and advanced Roman province, and this eastern section was not neglected. Trèves, situated somewhat to the east of our Lorraine, was a usual residence of the Emperor, and the palaces, arches and aqueducts built there were of a very high order—among the best specimens of Roman construction north of Italy. In various small places, as well as in Toul and Metz, there are splendid ruins. As can be seen by consulting the Peutinger Roman map (No. 2), roads were constructed in the region and were well maintained. Later comers from Rome tramped along these roads bringing their gifts. Before the fourth century Christianity had spread to the Moselle and the Meuse, and then there was established at Trèves a metropolitan bishop under whose jurisdiction were the bishops of Metz, Toul, and Verdun.

As Christianity pushed up from the south, it was met by new invasions from the north-east and east. The Suevi, no longer held in check by a Roman hand, crossed the Rhine and took up their abode on the left bank. Vandals, Burgundians, Huns, swept across the territory of Lorraine as they had swept over the Alsatian plain and mountains, laying waste Trèves, Metz, Verdun, and the smaller settlements. They were terrible visitors; yet a percentage of the population survived their raids, being maimed and injured but not exterminated. Trèves was sufficiently alive to call for a new circus, and Metz showed equal recuperative power after Attila's raid.

In the next epoch the actual proportion of Teutonic, Celtic, and other nationalities among the settlers in the Lorraine region becomes a moot question.[44]

---

[44] Scholars are not, indeed, agreed even as to the previous generalizations. Since 1871 German ethnologists have been inclined to rate the Germanic influence as dominant in Lorraine from Cesar's time, while French savants lay stress on the persistence of non-Teutonic traits.

It is very difficult to disentangle even the theories of the racial elements that persisted in Lorraine. Nor would a convincing solution be reached even with the decision of the linguistic question. No one can look at America without seeing at a glance that language does not necessarily indicate race. And in Europe, consider the Flemings, who, notwithstanding the fact that their Celtic ancestry seems assured, nevertheless speak a Germanic dialect, while the Walloons, blue eyed and fair haired, speak a Latin-based patois. Nor is there any more curious instance of the imposition of language and of nationality upon aliens than that effected by the Germans upon the people of Brandenburg and Prussia. An essentially Slavic and Lithuanian population was Germanized by colonists. How thoroughly this Germanization was carried out becomes apparent if one recalls that Treitschke, whose name is now familiar to everyone, was himself of Slavic origin.

For an approximate conclusion about the natives of Alsace-Lorraine, a conscientious investigator like Schoepflin[45] may be accepted as trustworthy, as this Alsatian scholar wrote in the eighteenth century when matters were finally at rest and long before the events of 1871 had thrown a partisan shadow across the statements of French and German scientists. He believes that one Germanic element affecting Lorraine came from an earlier immigration than that of the Suevi. Cæsar repulsed a fresh accession of newcomers, but he left the Nemetes near Spire, the Waugones near Woevre, and the Tribuces near Strasburg. In the fifth century these peoples completely abandoned their own idiom for Latin. The native soldiers, taken into the pay of Rome to aid against the other incoming Germans, learned Latin, stayed on the soil, and became the ancestors of a new composite race, which was crushed by the later invasions but never annihilated, not even by the devastating fury of Attila himself. In Lorraine, even more than in Alsace, three different strains of blood, Roman, Celtic, and German, contributed to the main stream of population, but the last-mentioned element was subordinate to the others. The chief point to remember is that some sections of the Teutonic race easily accepted certain portions of the Celto-Roman civilization, and some were little affected by their new environment.

---

[45] *Alsatia Illustrata.*

The later Germanic migration, the Alemanni and Frankish-Hessian peoples, whose Germanic origin was not effaced, settled apparently in the open country, leaving the cities to the continued occupation of the remnants of the Celto-Roman citizens, who impressed their language on the Germans who joined them. There remained a marked difference of speech between peasant and burgher. But in spite of local linguistic diversity, out of the union of the Germanic immigrants with the older families whom they found on the ground, sprang a distinctive race that by the tenth century felt itself a unit and had as marked an individuality as the other national nuclei of Central Europe. The ingredients remained visible in non-uniting traces of the characteristics distinguishing respectively the Germanic and the Celto-Roman elements. Yet the latter seemed dominant if one may judge from the kind of adjectives applied to the Lorraine character[46] in the chronicles of successive epochs. A military and chivalric spirit, sensitiveness, a tendency to religious phantasy, witty conversation,—are repeatedly mentioned as its attributes.

At the end of the sixth century monastic foundations began to be established and became very numerous between the Meuse and the Vosges. They were the centres of active industry. Forests were cleared, marshes drained, slavery put down, art and science saved for the world. These activities were due to the efforts of the Irish missionary Columba and his disciples, who came to Lorraine at this time. Other Irish monks followed and many religious houses were established. One Deodat felled forests, drained swamps, and left his name to a little hermitage from which sprang the city of St. Dié. Almost at the same period Gondelbert founded the abbey Senones, over which in the course of the eighteenth century presided as abbot Dom Calmet, the historian of Lorraine. Mighty estates were in the possession of these cloisters; some had as many as 1500 people under their care. They had fortifications to protect them from the onslaughts of the nobles. The inmates themselves could not bear arms; as a result they had in their pay armed men. There were thus at the service of abbots and abbesses many small independent military forces, able to confront the troops of warriors headed by the many nobles. Quarrels were many and petty warfare prevailed.

---

[46] "Études sur la Lorraine dite Allemande le pays Messin et l'ancienne province d'Alsace," par D. A. Godron, *Mém. de la société d'Archéologie de Lorraine*, 3d série vol. i., p. 255.

It was under the tradition of such influences that Jeanne d'Arc was born and grew up. Her natal village of Domremy was, to be sure, within the borders of Champagne, but only just across the Meuse on the lower watershed of the Vosges mountains, in a pastoral and wooded country. To all intents and purposes the mental and physical influences were the same as those of Lorraine, and the spirit of mysticism and religion spread abroad by Columba and his followers still hovered over the valley. Celtic myths, German minnesingers and romances, and the messages of the Irish monks, their sermons full of vivid imagery—all together had woven a web in which the peasant imagination was readily entangled.

II.

WHEN THE MAP WAS IN THE MAKING

LIKE the rest of Western Gaul and the Rhineland, Lorraine was comprised in the Carolingian Empire and only received its name after and by virtue of certain partitions of that Empire effected in 843 and later: *Lotharii regnum*, Lotharingen, Lorraine. The Treaty of Meersen, 870 A.D., which gave Alsace to Louis the German, left the major part of Lorraine under West Frankish sovereignty. The portion that retained the name passed back and forth several times between German and Frankish kings, as the Gallo-Roman element was sometimes dominant and sometimes dominated. The attempt of the *Loherains* to banish the German Zwentibold[47] failed, while again, in the first half of the tenth century they succeeded in attaching themselves to Louis d'Outremer of France. In 951, *Lotherregne* was divided into two duchies: Lower or Ripuarian Lorraine, reaching to the North Sea and including among other realms Holland; and Upper Lorraine, or Mosellana. Soon the name was applied only to this last-mentioned tract, which was the Duchy of Lorraine. There are very few historical documents pertaining to the early dukes prior to 1048, when Gerard d'Alsace succeeded his childless brother Albert and became the founder of the ducal line.

The feudal relation of this duchy is also a controversial point. M. Godron maintains that at no time did it or the Duchy of Bar belong, as an immediate fief, to France or to the Emperor. Bar was also a fragment of Lothaire's realm that finally became attached to Lorraine. The Dukes of Lorraine were, it is true, vassals of the Counts of Champagne, and thus mediate vassals of France for four or five towns and villages, and under this title they took part in the States-General. They were also vassals of the Holy Roman Empire for other fiefs of no great importance, and by virtue of that feudal lien frequently appeared at the Diets of Germany before the period when the number of

---

[47] Zwentibold was the illegitimate son of Emperor Arnulf. His creation of a realm for his son did not seem to imply its dependence either on Germany or France. It simply added another to the small kingdoms into which the great Frankish state had fallen. Emerton, p. 92.

electors was reduced. But in their ducal capacity the Lorraine sovereigns were free. The bishops of Toul, Metz, and Verdun were princes of the empire on behalf of their ecclesiastical sees, and they were quite independent of the ducal sovereigns in the midst of whose possessions their cities were located. From the eleventh century to the fifteenth there were fifteen ducal administrations,[48] all afflicted by petty wars between the rulers and their vassals and neighbours.

Ferri III. reigned for more than fifty years and deserves mention because during his rule the cities began to come to the fore as important factors in the affairs of Lorraine. Continued hostilities with the Bishop of Metz and with lesser nobles forced the Duke to turn for support to his own burghers. A marked impulse was given to the municipal movement through the privileges bestowed by Ferri in the hope of strengthening himself against the nobles by obtaining the friendship of the Third Estate. The majority of the municipal charters of Lorraine were modelled upon the charter of Beaumont in Argonne. In the church lands too the bishops found themselves forced to recognize the rising community spirit and to grant charters in their turn, but as a rule these charters were less favourable to the citizen than those of the Beaumont type.

Civic freedom, civic importance were tempting baits to towns-folk, who as individuals were impotent. Citizens were glad to be incorporated into a strong, chartered personality, and these same chartered personalities soon proved new Richmonds on the battlefields. Dating from the fourteenth century, the dukes found that they had unwittingly admitted to the body politic a formidable element, an element that could not safely be ignored. By that time the country was in a pathetic state of misery, as a result of its being continually harassed and down-trodden by warring parties. In the mid-century (1358), a class below that of the commoner, the peasants, had actually banded together, armed with any weapons they could pick up, and presented a united front to their oppressors. *Jacques Bonhomme* was the generic name for the peasant, and *Jacquerie* was the term applied to their angry though

---

[48] The dukes were: Theodoric II., the Valiant, 1069–1115; Simon, 1139; Matthieu, 1176; Simon II., 1205; Ferri, 1206; Ferri II., 1213; Thibaut, 1220; Matthieu II., 1251; Ferri III., 1304; Theobald II., 1312; Ferri IV., called the Struggler, 1328, Rudolph or Raoul, 1346; John, 1391; Charles II., or I., 1431.

feeble protests. They marched upon the châteaux, carrying stones, pitchforks, scythes, knives, and in many instances succeeded in raiding and pillaging the dwellings of the nobles in revenge for all they had suffered at the hands of the aristocracy.

Lorraine was not alone in being thus attacked from below. Other provinces suffered too. The crisis was short, not more than a few weeks in duration. The strength of the peasants was in their fury and that burned out quickly, leaving only sullen ashes of despair. The cities were a more sturdy force. The citizens were zealous to maintain the rights they had bought at high prices. Though suppressed again and again, the burghers showed recuperative force sufficient to make fresh protests as they gathered fresh vigour. The contest between one town, Neufchâteau, and the dukes of Lorraine was a terrible one, marked by frightful injuries and fierce reprisals. When, in 1390, Duke John died, his son Charles believed that he had been poisoned by order of the citizens of Neufchâteau, and Charles lost no time in inflicting condign punishment on the burghers. Nor was his anger expended at once. For over twenty years bitter enmity between him and the town continued. Neufchâteau was a French fief and Duke Charles was summoned to appear before the *parlement* and answer for his treatment of the burghers. This the Duke refused to do and the French Court passed an act exempting the inhabitants of Neufchâteau from the "jurisdiction, obedience, and subjection to the Duke of Lorraine and his successors and declaring them subjects of the King and his successors!" The Duke was also condemned to pay the King one thousand silver marks as a fine for his disobedience. But the mind of Charles VI. was already clouded and his next act was to restore the Duke to favour. As a result, Neufchâteau failed to secure independence.

The reign of this Charles of Lorraine differed from that of Ferri III. only in that its theatre of action was wider. He played a part in international affairs and also casually appears in the great drama of the repulse of the English, as he was at Nancy when Jeanne d'Arc went thither to visit the church of St. Nicolas du Port. Charles consented to a personal interview with the young girl. He even listened patiently to her adjuration to renounce his dissipated life and fight in the King's behalf. He excused himself on the score of his infirmities, but courteously expressed his gratitude for her interest and dismissed her kindly with gifts of a horse and money.

Shortly after this incident, in 1431, Charles died at Nancy and his duchy entered on still more troublous times. As he left no son to carry on the male line, his elder daughter, Isabella, married to René of Anjou, was declared his heir. Eighty-three nobles gave their oaths to support her accession and to recognize the Duchess of Anjou as *dame et souveraine*, with her husband as her coadjutor. The dukedom of Bar was among René's possessions, so it seemed as though one fruitful source of misery for the land would be exorcised by this new régime, since quarrels between the Dukes of Bar and Lorraine had brought frequent calamities. The dying Duke took further precautions to ensure tranquillity by asking the cities to approve the innovation of accepting a female ruler. It was the first time that the Third Estate had been recognized as having any political significance in Lorraine, such recognition being the natural sequence of the civil liberty inaugurated by the provisions of the charter of Beaumont. That liberal charter was regarded as the desirable model by all communities when asking incorporated privileges, but not all communities were fortunate enough to wrest its articles, or their equivalent, from their overlords.

René and Isabella were very lavish in their offers to the nobles, the clergy, and the cities of Lorraine. To the last mentioned they assured the maintenance of all the rights and privileges they had ever enjoyed. Signatures seemed cheap payment for support of a contested inheritance, but the scraps of paper they validated were held up as landmarks for future guidance by the party of the second part, a very tenacious party. From that epoch on, each new duke was compelled to follow a precedent once inaugurated, and the cities were very determined in forcing the fulfilment of pledges made to them when the suzerain was the person obliged.

Isabella soon found that the allegiance of the people of Lorraine was not sufficient to ensure her peaceful enjoyment of her paternal inheritance. Her father had had a brother, the Duke of Vaudemont, that brother had a son, Anthony, who protested that a male fief was a thing that could not lightly be set aside by the mere acquiescence of vassals. His first protests fell flat. Isabella and her husband were invested with the sovereignty in spite of the counter claims. Then a neighbour, the great Duke of Burgundy, became interested in the controversy and aided Anthony to assert himself, while the French King gave assistance to Isabella and René. The two forces met at Bulgnéville and, by the arbitrament of arms, Anthony was quickly proved right. In fifteen minutes, the battle was decided in his favour, so says an *imperial* report, because the new artillery of his Burgundian ally outweighed the skill of Duke René. Three thousand Lorrainers lay dead upon the field. René himself was taken prisoner and it was six years before he was liberated. Diplomacy, however, was in favour of Isabella. At Basel, in April, 1434, the Emperor Sigismund pronounced his approval of her accession to her father's duchy, woman though she was, but he was not in a position to enforce his opinion on the European world. The French King also supported Isabella, and brought his troops to Metz, but failed to obtain any success by his efforts. Matters rested in debate until an alliance was formed between the contestants by the marriage of young Yolande, daughter of Isabella, to Frederick, son of Anthony. King René never took much part in the administration of his wife's duchy. When he regained his freedom, he left that duty to her while he devoted himself to making good his claim to Naples, and to the patronage of art and literature in Provence. After Isabella's death in 1453, René's sons were, nominally, at the head of affairs in Lorraine, but they were courtiers in attendance upon the French King rather than sovereigns in their own behalf, and played little part in the duchy. At the death of Nicolas in 1473, the Lorraine-Anjou line became extinct and the next of kin was young René II., son of Yolande and Frederick of Vaudemont, who thus united in his own person the titles of Vaudemont, Bar, and Lorraine.

In 1473, the year of René's accession, the existence of the duchy—an independent unit—was menaced by a notable attempt to make a new realm in Europe.

III.

THE ASPIRATIONS OF BURGUNDY

AS already mentioned in the story of Alsace, Charles, Duke of Burgundy, sovereign over a group of Netherland duchies, countships, and seigniories, in addition to his two Burgundies, conceived the idea of welding the congeries into a regal unity, on the plan of the "Middle Kingdom,"—*Lotharii regnum*—of the ninth century. The northern group had grown in compactness by various methods of "annexation" effected during his father's lifetime. Charles wished to do more than annex: he wished to *create* a new European power, and the Emperor was not unwilling to invest him with the coveted dignity. But in addition to obtaining a title, Charles wished to attain continuity for his territory. The opportunity offered of taking Upper Alsace had been a welcome chance to fill in part of the chasm between the Burgundies and the Netherlands. He had thought of an alliance between his daughter Mary and Nicolas of Lorraine as a means of throwing Lorraine into the same chasm. Other plans had banished this one before the death of Nicolas in 1473. After that event and after René's accession, another scheme occurred to the ambitious Duke.

As soon as the death of Nicolas left the dukedom vacant, Yolande of Anjou-Vaudemont[49] had hastened to Nancy with her son René II. to claim the heritage. She obtained recognition and then abdicated in favour of René who was duly acknowledged as Duke of Lorraine. But neither the new Duke nor his mother felt very secure in their tenure. Among their noble vassals were many who had been in close relations with Charles of Burgundy, admiring him as the one strong man of Europe, able to hold his own against the impoverished Emperor Frederick III. and Louis XI., King of France, who was just beginning to be aggressive. Lorraine was but a little strip of land between bigger neighbours, and powerful friends were very necessary for her comfort and well-being.

---

[49] Yolande's sister was the unfortunate Margaret of Anjou, wife of Henry VI. of England.

Under the influence of the group of Burgundian partisans, one of the first acts of the new administration was an alliance, offensive and defensive, between René and Charles. The latter was to be "Protector" of Lorraine with freedom to march his armies over the land at will. As reward for his "protection" René pledged himself to appoint officials "bound by oath to the Duke of Burgundy," thus planting the adherents of Charles firmly within his land and household. Moreover, the more important of these officers were expressly released from fidelity to René in case he abandoned Burgundian interests. Yolande endorsed the articles of the pact and so did seventy-four of the Lorraine nobles, November 18, 1473. This act might seem to evince a very strange readiness to deliver over the duchy to external authority. But there was a natural timidity on the part of the young and untried sovereign and a distrust of his ability on the part of the vassals.

At first, René was much attracted towards Charles. It was the fascination naturally felt by a youth of twenty for a man of forty, in all the flush of successful middle-life. But little by little Charles became inordinately exigent, and René's admiration waned under the annoyance of Burgundian aggression. The visitors did not rest content with what had been pledged to them, liberal as were the provisions of the compact. In many towns not specified, Lorraine garrisons were replaced by Burgundian. There was increasing fear on the part of the inhabitants lest the "protecting" hand might prove an oppressive one. René chafed under the strain and finally broke the alliance. On April 18, 1475, less than two years after his accession, he joined the League of Constance,—a confederation of foes[50] to Burgundy,—and abjured the protection he had once gladly accepted.

There was a touch of old King René's taste for dramatic effect in his grandson's fashion of declaring war upon Charles. His herald rode up to a gorgeous tent of red velvet and was admitted to the Burgundian Duke's presence. The first view of "Le Téméraire" was so terrifying to the peaceful herald that he delivered his letter in frightened silence and then, without further preliminaries, threw down the blood-stained gauntlet that he had been bidden offer as a gage to open hostilities, and uttered his formal message[51]:

---

[50] The reason for the hostility of the Swiss to the Duke of Burgundy is another story.

[51] *Bulletin de l'acad. royal de Belgique*, 1887.

> To thee, Charles of Burgundy, in behalf of the very high, etc., Duke of Lorraine, my lord, I announce defiance with fire and blood against thee, thy countries, thy subjects, thy allies, and further charge have I none.

The reply was, in part:

> Herald, I have heard the exposition of thy charge, whereby thou hast given me cause for joy, and, to show you how matters are, thou shalt wear my robe with this gift. Thou shalt tell thy master that I will be in his land very speedily and that my greatest fear is that I may not find him there.

René depended on Louis XI. to aid him in making good his words and it was a grievous disappointment to him that the French King found it convenient just then to make a peace with Burgundy for nine years, wholly disregarding his young friend's pressing needs. René received some assistance from the city of Strasburg and from other foes to Burgundy, but it was insufficient to prevent the entry of Charles into Nancy, where he actually received homage, not as protector, but as sovereign duke. The pacification of Lorraine was a matter of profound importance to the Duke of Burgundy at that moment. His star was in the ascendant and he saw his projected kingdom almost as a realization. This particular duchy was a keystone to his structure, and it was important to his success not to alienate its people. Accordingly, he acted the rôle of a merciful conqueror. No cruelty was permitted, and a diplomatic, conciliatory policy was rigidly adhered to. The majority of the Lorrainers were apparently prepared to surrender the cause of the legitimate heir, and accepted the new order of things without further protests. At the end of December, Charles convened the Estates of Lorraine in the ducal palace, addressed them as his subjects, promised to be a just sovereign, demanded their affection, set forth his plans of territorial expansion, and announced his intention of making Nancy the capital of his united states. The Emperor had shown himself in complete accord with the Duke's ambitions, René seemed almost destitute, and there was every prospect of a new régime being inaugurated upon the ruins of the House of Lorraine. When on January 11th Charles left Nancy, he issued a grandiloquent manifesto declaring that he was now ready to punish the Swiss for all the wrongs inflicted upon their neighbours, as well as all who had dared to invade his province of Burgundy. These were the allies upon whom the dispossessed René threw himself, deserted as he was by Louis XI. Confident of their assistance, he succeeded in addition in rallying many Lorrainers again to his standard, and when, nearly a year later, Charles attempted to return to the city that had permitted him to exercise certain sovereign rights, he found the gates closed and no knocking sufficed to open them. By that time the battle of Granson had been fought, and he had learned the strength of the victorious Swiss mountaineers in that terrible defeat of his trained troops.

> Item, the Duke of Burgoyne hath conquered Lorreyn [writes Sir John Paston in a newsy letter dated March 21, 1476], and Queen Margreet shall nott nowe be lykelyhod have it . . . but after this conquest off Lorreyne the Duke toke grete corage to goo upon the londe off the Swechys [Swiss] to conquer them butt they berded hym at an onsett place and hath dystrussyd hym and hathe slayne the most part of his vanwarde and wonne all hys ordynnaunce and artylrye and mor ovyr all stuffe that he hade in hys ost with hym . . . and soo men deme hys pryde is abatyd. Men tolde hym that they were ffrowarde karlys butte he wolde nott beleve it and yitt men seye that he woll to them ageyn.[52]

The last year of the life of Charles was full of disasters from which he failed to extricate himself. Possibly by the time he had returned to Nancy he was half maddened by disappointment. The world was going so ill with him! It was not only force that he had to contend with, but treachery. The defection of certain Italian allies on the very eve of the battle before the unopened gates of Nancy, was the last straw to his misfortunes. Meantime René had gained substantial ground. An opportune private legacy enabled him to pay his troops, a Swiss Diet at Freiburg approved a closer alliance with him, and Louis XI., while ostensibly maintaining his truce with Charles, had intimated that a French army would be on hand in Dauphiné, "ready to help adjust the affairs of Savoy," and had furthermore been very gracious to a Swiss embassy. René did not feel, therefore, quite friendless. The garrison left by Charles at Nancy readily capitulated to René, and when Charles reached Lorraine, he found he could command no base except Pont-à-Mousson, and that his first pleasant experience at Nancy was not to be repeated. On October 22d, the Burgundian invested the city that he intended to make his new capital. It was a siege

---

[52] *The Paston Letters*, v., p. 258.

marked by much hardship for both contestants. Charles was harried from without, the burghers were starved within the city, but both besiegers and besieged held out bravely, the latter staunch from terror of Burgundian cruelties and buoyed up by the hope of René's arrival with reinforcements. René came at last and the battle was fought on January 5th. An effective contingent of Swiss troops had proceeded across Alsace from Basel, consuming a week in the march, to reinforce René's body of Lorrainers and Alsatians. Charles was urged by his advisers not to risk battle but to let cold and hunger be his allies until the resources of the young Duke, meagre at the best, were exhausted. *Le Téméraire* refused to listen to this suggestion. His failure to do so resulted in an overwhelming defeat. Charles lost his life, being found, almost naked, in a pool of water. His one-time youthful adorer is said to have shown what honour he could to the wretched remains of his crushed foe. For five days the body lay in state before the high altar of the Church of St. George and a long train of Lorraine nobles, led by the young Duke himself, followed the coffin to the place of burial where it lay for a time, later to be transferred to Bruges.

With the death of Charles of Burgundy, Lorraine missed the fate of being the heart of a brand-new kingdom and again took her place on the map of Europe as a duchy, yet henceforth, a duchy more closely allied to French interests than it had been hitherto.

IV.

THE NEW LEARNING

FOR thirty years, René II. held the sovereignty in Lorraine. He had rather hoped to extend that sovereignty by the addition of certain fragments of the Burgundian group of lands, shattered in their cohesiveness because Charles's daughter, Mary, was debarred from male fiefs, while she was accepted as successor to all of her father's duchies, countships, and seigniories not under the Salic law. Luxemburg and Burgundy were temptingly close to Lorraine—so easily annexable! Territorial expansion required, however, more skill and more force to accomplish than the Duke of Lorraine could command. Louis XI. was a better hand at the game. He took charge of the duchy of Burgundy, while the Franche-Comté remained within the Empire. René achieved no territorial gains and, indeed, almost lost what had been saved for him because of the King's zeal to reach the Rhine, which he called the "natural boundary" of France. Louis XI. was quite willing to disregard ducal palings that obstructed his course, but he failed to accomplish his desire.

But if René had not the aggressive political ability to increase the area of his domain, the reputation of Lorraine was certainly enhanced by his receptivity to new ideas and to the renascence of learning as it surged towards the duchy from both Germany and France. The fantastic King René I. had bequeathed to his grandson gentle scholarly tastes, and René II. lived in a time when, and in a region where, new thoughts were buzzing about like bees. The cities lying along the international highways over which the disciples of new culture passed were keen to hear their messages. The Rhinelands were the cradle of many precious incunabula, the first fruits of the printing-presses set up at Strasburg in Alsace, and at St. Dié in Lorraine, and the little groups of earnest seekers after truth that gathered about these presses were very active minded and intelligent scholars, zealous for knowledge of every kind that pertained to man—to Humanism.

St. Dié was the seat of the monastery founded by Deodat in the seventh century, when the Irish monks were spreading their message abroad in

Lorraine. The town that grew up on the spot enjoyed *immediaté* to Emperor and Pope and thus was legally independent of the sovereign by whose territories it was encircled, but that fact was lost sight of when the friendship of the Duke offered pleasant relations and practical advantages. The working scholars, the humanists at St. Dié were definitely associated into a guild under the name of *Gymnasium Vogense*, the presiding genius of the circle being René's own secretary, Walter Ludd, whose ability to find means to finance publishing enterprises attracted to St. Dié kindred spirits, anxious for a public.

Among these literary and technical collaborators were Philesius Ringmann, Joh. Basius Sendacurius, and Martin Waldseemüller. The last mentioned was, apparently, a universal genius. In a memorial to Duke René he calls himself a *clerc du diocèse de Cōstance*, as well as *imprimeur*. Thus he was already in theological orders before coming to Lorraine as a skilled printer. There he held office as Canon of St. Dié until his death in 1522. To posterity, however, Martin Waldseemüller is known in his capacity as cartographer and as part editor of a notable edition of Ptolemy's great work on geography, and as sponsor for the name of *America*.

Among all the sciences that stormed the strongholds of European ignorance at the end of the fifteenth and the beginning of the sixteenth century, geography was, perhaps, the most striking apparition. It represented new demands for accuracy, for applied knowledge based upon acquired data. Ptolemy had had for many centuries a surprising vogue and prestige. There are few scholars who have commanded implicit adherence to their example during as long a period as did Claudius Ptolemæus, the second-century Alexandrian geographer. For over a thousand years his *Cosmographia* was the one and only geographical authority available. Successive editions contained fresh matter, and after a time maps were added to illustrate the text. Nevertheless, there was a singular timidity on the part of editors and cosmographers. They were afraid to make the slightest statement without sheltering themselves under the magic name of Ptolemy, even when the points they advanced could not have been dreamed of in his philosophy. This same servility manifested itself in the copying of the earlier maps when maps began to be given as illustrations to the printed text (1478). That of Germany is attributed to an original by an Alexandrian of the fifth century. For, in addition to the Peutinger map, 200 (?) A.D., there are many other loose sheet MS. representations of Northern Europe found scattered through monasteries and libraries. Some are weird productions like those made by the Greek monks of Mount Athos, some are mythical, and others show crude efforts to attain the actual outline. That used as a basis of the Ptolemy of 1478 belongs to the last group. Poor as it was, it was reinserted in several editions, until finally replaced by Waldseemüller's notable new cut made for the Strasburg edition of 1513. Thus Germany was not put on the map in a recognizable form until the Alsatian-Lorraine group became interested in the subject. The maps of 1513 were the first real contribution towards the cartographical reformation preceding the inauguration of modern geography by Mercator and Ortelius in 1569–1570.

The Strasburg Ptolemy contained twenty new, in addition to the twenty-seven old, maps of previous issues. That representing Germany marks a wonderful advance towards a correct cartographical conception and, during more than half a century, was used as a model for reproductions. This is considered the work of Martin Waldseemüller. There is also an attempt at representing local geography for which he is probably responsible. A whole sheet is devoted to the delineation of the contour and outlines of "Lorraine," a natural compliment to the ducal friend who was financing the enterprise. The result of scanty knowledge, it could not be accepted as a tourist's guide, but it marks, nevertheless, a distinct epoch in cartography.

The Ptolemy with its atlas was long in the making, and bears only the names of the later collaborators who completed its production in the Alsatian imperial city and dedicated it to Emperor Maximilian. But there is another little volume closely identified with Lorraine, that made its appearance six years earlier. In 1507, Martinus Ilacomilus, as the versatile scholar liked to Græcize his German Waldseemüller, published at St. Dié a little introduction to cosmography, to which was added a Latin version of the four letters of Americus Vespuccius, translated from the French version of the original. Philesius Ringmann and Sendacurius collaborated in the enterprise, the latter being the translator, and the former contributing some poems to soften the hard lines of scientific fact. The letters had been dedicated to a schoolmate of the discoverer, but the translator felt quite free to turn that dedication to the service of Duke René, although the substance of the lines failed to apply to the patron of Lorraine.⁵³ Little slips of that nature did not trouble the literary conscience of the day. Sources were not scanned too severely, so that fresh knowledge bubbled up attractively. That news of the explorers came to the Rhinelands in uncertain ways, is evident from the fact that Lorraine scholars were ignorant of Columbus as late as 1507. It is Waldseemüller who makes the explicit suggestion that the name of the fourth part of the world might properly be made out of the name of Americus Vespuccius, turned into a feminine form to correspond with *Asia* and *Europa*, both named from women.⁵⁴

Upon his great map of America, designed to accompany his little treatise, Waldseemüller, accordingly, placed the name "America," and on the map it stayed for good and all, although the originator desired to take it off when he learned more about Columbus. He was not the kind of man who fears to acknowledge a mistake, but he could not utter what he did not know. His book and his map had had a wonderful vogue. The information that they had spread over the world could not be recalled, and "America" the designation remained for all time. In 1508, the cosmographer refers to the wide circulation of his work with pardonable pride. Little by little his misconceptions were corrected. They could readily be set aright, for they sprang from lack of opportunity to know, not from contentment with a false vision of things.

René's interest extended to literature and the fine arts as well as to the pursuits of the Gymnasium Vogense. His patronage stimulated both poetry and painting. In his lifetime an artistic movement started that continued under his successors, making Lorraine take rank among the cultivated little states of Europe. In regard to the poets of St. Dié, writing in Latin, a friendly

---

⁵³ It might be added that there have been attempts to make them apply and to prove that as a child René might have gone to Italy with his father and been placed under the tutelage of the elder Vespuccio, who was the instructor of his nephew, Amerigo.

⁵⁴ He refers twice to the point in his *Cosmographicæ Introductio:* . . . "& quarta orbis pars (quam quia Americus invenit Amerigen/quasi Americi terrā/sive Americā nuncupate licet)" (p. xxv.); and "Nunc vero & hæ partes sunt lustratæ/& aha quarta pars per Americũ vesutiũ (ut in sequentibus audietur) inventa est/quā non video cur quis vetet ab Americo inventore sagacis ingenii viro Amerigen quasi Americi terrā/sive Americam dicendā; cũ & Europa & Asia a mulieribus sua sortita sint nomina." Herbermann, *Waldseemüller's Cosmographiæ Introductio* (New York, 1908).

critic declares that they were not inferior to Virgil, a dictum with which the more acute Dom Calmet, ardent Lorrainer though he was, did not agree.

Apart from its intellectual life, the duchy gained prestige during René's administration because the grouping together of Lorraine, Bar, and Vaudemont resulted in an increased territorial unity. Furthermore, René had succeeded in subordinating several of the free cities and bringing them partially under ducal sway, or at least into harmonious relations with it. The sees also became, practically, domains of the House of Lorraine because of family ties between dukes and bishops.

MAP NO. 6
Waldseemüller's Map of Germany, 1505.
(From Ptolemy of 1513)

V.

THE HOUSE OF LORRAINE IN EUROPE

IN 1508, just when Waldseemüller was rejoicing over the circulation of his new map and "America" was making itself known, René II. died, leaving five sons, who were all provided with fractions of the paternal seigniories. To Anthony, the eldest, was bequeathed the sovereignty of Lorraine, Bar, and Vaudemont, under the express stipulation that the territory should be kept intact, and no portion alienated. Another son, Claude, received the countship of Guise. Later he became naturalized in France, and Francis I. turned his countship into a dukedom, thus founding the powerful family that played such a prominent part in French politics. The inclination manifested by René for France, in spite of the bad faith he had experienced in his relations with Louis XI., was continued by his sons. The exact status of the duchy was still not fixed. At the Diet of Worms, 1492, René had rendered homage to Maximilian but refused to take the oath sworn by the German princes.[55] Anthony, brought up in the French court under the eyes of Louis himself, was even more Gallicized than his father. He gained some renown through his suppression of the revolt of the Alsatian peasants, known as *Rustauds*, when the disaffection spread into Lorraine. That episode, with its disastrous results to the unhappy rustics, has already been referred to in recounting the story of Alsace. It was one of the manifestations of unrest and despair among the oppressed classes that were intermittent precursors of the greater convulsion of the French Revolution. Anthony defeated these peasant bands in two regular engagements, victories that were to be expected, for he had skill on his side, and they only helpless hate on theirs.

As regards Lorraine, the real importance of Anthony's administration was the stand he took in asserting the practical independence of his duchy from imperial control, even though he yielded some points and accepted certain promises. After several protests against interference in the domestic affairs of Lorraine—protests which had been initiated by Duke René in 1492—Duke

---

[55] Godron, *Études sur la Lorraine*, p. 277.

Anthony sent his representative to take part in a formal agreement between the electors of the Empire and Ferdinand, then still King of the Romans. At this gathering, known as the Convention of Nuremberg (August 26, 1542), among other questions debated was that of the relation between Lorraine and the Empire. Probably many of the princes were more or less reluctant to accept their assessment, even when they acknowledged their feudal obligations. But it was the *obligation* that Duke Anthony denied. He declared that he was vassal to the Emperor in behalf of a few seigniories only, and that Lorraine was a free and independent state. He claimed immunity from regular imperial charges and resented the fact that judges of the Imperial Chamber had brought action against him and his subjects by "*appellations* and *mandemens*"—something hitherto unheard of, as he could prove, if necessary. The statement continues:

> Nevertheless, as he wished to live in peace and good relations with the emperor, the princes, and the electors, he [Anthony] consented to contribute a certain sum annually, on account of the fiefs which he held from the Empire incorporated in and united to his duchy, and to pay a share in the taxes and contributions levied on the members of the Empire, on condition that his duchy of Lorraine should be under the protection of the Empire on the same par as the other Estates and members which held from it, and that the tax should be moderate and proportionate to the small amount of revenue that he drew from his Imperial fiefs, so that it should not be too heavy a burden on him and the dukes, his successors.
>
> For these reasons, Ferdinand I., King of the Romans, in the name of the Emperor, Charles V., his brother, replied that the duchy of Lorraine was subject to the Empire; that nevertheless, to be favourable to Duke Anthony, the King Ferdinand, in the name of the Emperor, his brother, and with the consent of the electors and members of the Empire, would receive not only the fiefs that he held from the Empire, but also his duchy of Lorraine and his seigniories of Blamont and of Pont-à-Mousson and others, under the protection of the Empire, provided that the duke and his successors should pay to the Imperial Chamber two thirds of the tax of an elector; that is to say, if an elector were taxed at 300 florins, the duke should pay 200; *au moyen de qui* the duchy of Lorraine was declared sovereignly free and independent.

The phrasing in the treaty is more exact and expressive than this analysis, given by Dom Calmet, in relation to the duchy of Lorraine: "Ducatus

Lotharingiæ cum suis appertinentibus Liber et non Incorporabilis Ducatus erit et manebit semper." And to make it still more emphatic these expressions are repeated *three times*.

This transaction was confirmed by the Emperor Charles V. at Spire, July 28, 1543, and accepted by the Imperial Chamber of Spire, August 29, 1561 renewed and confirmed by Emperor Rudolph at Prague, January 2, 1603, as well as by the electors on each occasion.

It would seem clear[56] that the status of Lorraine was recognized as a peculiar one, and that Ferdinand, as representative of the Emperor, acknowledged this peculiarity, made allowance in the tax assessment, and promised that existing conditions should be maintained, and that neither the duchy nor any of its parts should be annexed to the Empire.

As a matter of fact, neither before nor after this Convention of 1542 did the dukes of Lorraine receive protection from the Holy Roman Empire. When danger was averted from the dukedom it was always due to other aid. Poor Lorraine, she was a tempting mark for many attacks!

Duke Anthony kept fairly neutral and avoided collision alike with the Emperor and the King. His brothers were French, his daughter-in-law, Christine, niece to the Emperor, so that his interests were divided. He died in 1544 and his son Francis followed him to the grave in 1546, just as he was negotiating a peace between the Emperor and Francis I. Then the problem presented by the division of interests in a buffer state became apparent. The guardianship of Christine, the widow, over her young son, Charles III., was viewed with suspicion because she was closely related to the great Habsburg, Charles V. Therefore the guardianship was transferred to the boy's uncle, the bishop of Metz, a French sympathizer. Probably that was the main reason why Henry II. of France found it so easy to possess himself of the three bishoprics,

---

[56] The clearness is not evident to all. Opposite meanings are read out of Dom Calmet's text (not available in Washington) by Herr von Sybel on the one side and MM. Mihiel and Godron on the other—the former considering that Lorraine's dependence on, the latter her independence of, the Empire is definitely stated. The opinion of M. Godron seems the most conclusive. (The date of the Convention as given by von Sybel is certainly wrong. It was 1542, not 1539.) See *Deutschlands Recht auf Elsass und Lothringen*, Heinrich von Sybel, Berlin, 1871 and "Études sur la Lorraine dite Allemande," D. A. Godron, *Mém. de la soc. d'archéologie*, Lorraine, 1874, p. 252. The citations from Dom Calmet are taken from this latter article, a careful and scholarly examination of the subject.

Metz, Toul, and Verdun, as he did in 1552, without the shedding of a drop of blood.

By the mid-fifteenth century, a strange state of political and theological confusion prevailed in the Empire. Many Lutheran princes had found the idea of autocracy over spiritual matters in their own domains quite fascinating, and a goodly number asserted their privileges, naturally to the disapproval of the Emperor. He considered that the harmony of the Empire was disturbed, and they counted him tyrannical when he tried to restrain their zeal. Accordingly, Maurice, Elector of Saxony, headed a mutiny against imperial authority. The protesting body actually applied to the King of France to save them from their own chief. At first Henry II. and these Lutheran princes were very chary about committing their thoughts to documents, fearful lest incriminating scraps of paper might prove inconvenient witnesses if the movement were not successful. But at last a compact was signed at Chambord, October 9, 1551. The purpose of the alliance was that of restoring liberty to the German fatherland (*pro Germaniæ patriæ libertate recuperanda*). In return for financial aid, the confederates were to refrain from opposing the French King in his projected seizure of Metz, Toul, and Verdun. The objective was not stated as baldly as that. The particular places menaced were covered by a phrase referring to cities not of Germanic speech. The champions of German liberty had to hedge considerably in joining forces with the Christian King.

As the Duke of Lorraine was a minor and removed from the charge of his mother, the Emperor's niece, the interests of his duchy, closely involved with the fate of these cities, were in the hands of his guardian, the bishop of Metz, who was thus free to exert himself in behalf of the French King if so inclined. And it was in that direction that his sympathies lay. The kinsfolk of his ward had become part and parcel of the French aristocracy, during the decades that had elapsed since Claude, the son of René II., had changed his county to a duchy and married Antoinette of Bourbon. Ten children, born of this marriage, took high rank in the realm. Two sons were cardinals; a third was Duke of Guise, and a fourth Duke of Aumale; one daughter married James V. of Scotland, and became mother to Mary, Queen of Scots, while the matrimonial alliances of the remaining children added prestige to the Lorraine House of Guise. It is, therefore, not improbable that the bishop did not oppose the entry of Henry II. into his see. But he was not the supreme authority there. Metz was not wrested from the bishop any more than it was snatched from the Emperor. It was wrested from its own municipal sovereignty. The city state had enjoyed great freedom for many long years. The citizens had frequently declared that they could not be constrained to support imperial wars in which they were not interested, nor would they accept papal orders unquestioned, notwithstanding the fact that their city was an episcopal seat. Respecting one of the bulls, they asserted stoutly that it was neither equitable nor just, adding that equity was a convenience not to be neglected.[57]

In the fifteenth and sixteenth centuries Metz was governed by municipal magistrates elected freely in the city and without any sensible control from the Empire. She levied her troops for defence, received embassies, signed treaties with dukes, counts, and kings. The lien that attached her to the Empire was very shadowy, *de facto*. The nominal feudal relation meant very little. When the emperors visited Metz, as most of them did from time to time, the city fathers were very dictatorial as to what provision they would furnish their self-invited guests, besides stipulating how many attendants might enter within the gates. Nor did blandishments and compliments avail to turn them from their decision. The visitors were the obliged party, not the civic host. At the moment of its capture, Metz was weakened by being cleft into two parties,—Catholic and Protestant, the former inclined towards Charles V. and the latter to Henry II. For private reasons the bishop espoused the cause of the latter, as he wanted to gain some prestige from the eminent position of the Lorraine cadet branch. He was the head of the conspirators against the city's independence, who pledged themselves to make the French entry smooth and easy. The citizens were deceived into thinking that the French King wished only a passage through their streets and were then soothed into submission by various arguments. It was on Palm Sunday that Montmorency knocked at the gate. The *coup d'état* that followed was quietly accomplished and the old *Reichstadt* passed from self-government to subordination without the shedding of a drop of blood.

---

[57] "Que cette bulle ne semble point être raisonable, ne fondée en équité. Car équité est une convenance de choses, laquelle requiert droit paireil en paireille et semblable cause." Godron quotes this from *Les chroniques de la ville de Metz*, p. 288.

Toul, also, was gained without a blow, and finally Lorraine at large was attacked by the seizure of the small Duke, who was carried off to Paris to be educated and thus attached to French sympathies like his cousins.

Henry II. tried in like manner to occupy Strasburg, in Alsace, but that city had not been prepared beforehand by local French sympathizers. The King was told that the French troops must not come within cannon shot of the walls—the range was shorter in that day than now—and that the King could not bring more than forty attendants into the city. Rabutin, one of the royal suite, writes that he could not describe Strasburg because he was not allowed to enter it, adding: "The inhabitants of this country are proud and haughty because they are not charged and burdened with exactions and are not accustomed to see men-at-arms in their beds."[58]

Anti-imperialism was all very well but there was a natural disinclination to become pro-French.

The Emperor did not accept this attack upon imperial fiefs with equanimity and resignation. The last vigorous effort made by Charles V. was his attempt to draw Metz back into the circle of the Empire. From October to January his troops—a collection of Flemings, Germans, and Italians, disagreeing bitterly among themselves—laid siege to the place. Charles and his sister, Mary of Hungary, the regent of the Netherlands, were both in the field, accompanied by the best of their commanders, but winter weather and the skill or good luck of the Duke of Guise, to whom was entrusted the defence of the besieged city, baffled them.

There is a tradition that Charles, seeing the siege a failure, called Fortune a fickle maid because she preferred a young king to an old emperor. Old he felt beyond the claim of his fifty-two years, and in this crisis he certainly lost confidence in his star. On January 1st he beat a retreat, only 12,000 out of 60,000 men being still in good condition, while the French had lost the small total of 250 officers and men. At least that was the number estimated by Guise, but his calculation may possibly have been influenced by partisan considerations. He also declared that all the wounded men, abandoned by the imperial forces, were carefully nursed back to health by the French. This defeat was one of the circumstances that prompted Charles V. to lay down his

---

[58] Lavisse, v^2., p. 150.

crown. Upon his abdication in 1555, he retired to Spain to find peace for his soul in the monastery of San Yuste, while to his son Philip II. was bequeathed the task of finding peace for Europe. There was a clamour for peace at any price by the people of all the states involved, and the price paid by the conferring statesmen was the practical abandonment of every gain that had been made in about half a century of intermittent hostilities.

"As to the restoration of Metz, Toul, and Verdun," wrote Cardinal Granvelle, one of the negotiators on behalf of Philip II., "we touched on that subject at Lille and I think my colleagues will be unanimous about returning to the subject *if* it be brought up at the negotiations even though nothing be obtained." When the treaty was signed at Cateau-Cambrésis on April 3, 1559, it was plain that nothing was obtained. There was not a single reference to the cities. With the abdication of Charles V., the imperial interests were severed from the inheritance of his son. Ferdinand, the brother of Charles, became Emperor without falling heir to the prestige of his predecessor. The cities of Lorraine remained with France, virtually by default. Philip only pressed their release to save his face with his kin across the Rhine. He really did not care for their fate. Discussion of the matter did not stop, indeed, with the consummation of the treaty. Emperor Ferdinand made several feeble attempts to assert imperial rights, but nothing came of embassies, negotiations, and reference to the Diet. The Lorraine family was a numerous and a powerful one in France, and all its members were glad to have three strong points of the duchy definitely allied to the French crown. Metz, Toul, and Verdun became French provincial towns.[59]

The influence of the Lorraine cardinals was also strong enough to retain possession of the minor Duke of Lorraine, Charles III., to marry him to Claude, a daughter of Henry II., and to bring him up as a good Frenchman. He had a long life, reigning as Duke for sixty-four years, but he had little to do with the Empire. He was a fervent Catholic, as was natural for a nephew of the Cardinal of Lorraine, and established a seat of learning at Pont à Mousson to further the ecclesiastical reforms that he espoused. This university was to be a bulwark against the disintegrating power of many creeds, such as were

---

[59] See Ruble, A., *Le traité de Cateau-Cambrésis, 1559*, Paris, 1889. The treaty was futile in most of its provisions, but the one great French asset in addition to this tacit acquiescence was England's cession of Calais. England was dislodged from that foothold at last.

affecting Germany. Charles entrusted the execution of his scheme to eleven Jesuits, who were ready to open the doors of the university in 1573. The first rector was a Scotchman, Edmund Hay, and the first chancellor, John Hay. By 1603 there were fifteen hundred students[60] of all nations.

Charles also effected reforms in the administration of justice in Lorraine. A queer jumble of laws and precedents and customs prevailed in the duchy, there being many local differences of procedure. These were codified, simplified, and unified. Another reform was that of the calendar. In this case, too, much confusion existed. Some religious establishments were in the habit of dating their year from March 25th, some from Christmas, and others from Easter. Charles, in an ordinance of November 15, 1579, ordered all documents, judicial acts, etc., to date from December 31st, as the last day of the year. Three years later he sanctioned the adoption of the Gregorian Calendar,—a reform very gradually accepted in different countries. Russia did not use the new style of calendar until a year or two ago. As a reward for services to his uncle, Charles IX., the Duke obtained the right of coinage and a few other royal privileges in his French fiefs. He tried to introduce a degree of absolutism in his duchy, but was forced by his nobles to relinquish such efforts. The privileges of the aristocracy were held to tenaciously in Lorraine, more so than elsewhere.

There is no doubt that the duchy gained in unity and prestige at this time. Had the son of Duke Charles been acknowledged as the successor to Henry III., the last of the Valois kings, by right of his mother Claude, the House of Lorraine would have founded a new dynasty. But attempts to attain this succession failed, and Henry of Navarre came to the throne.[61]

In 1608, Charles III. died, and was succeeded by his son Henry, whose only child was a daughter. There was an attempt to prove that the Salic law did not obtain in Lorraine. To make his title sure, however, the male heir married

---

[60] One Vitry (*Hist. occidental*) is not very flattering in his references to the students in the little university. He calls the English cowardly and fond of wine, the French proud and effeminate, the German *furibonds* and coarse in conversion, the Burgundians brutal, the Lombardians avaricious, the Romans seditious and violent, while the Flemish are extravagant and wasteful, loving luxury, good eating, and dissipation!

[61] Sully says that Duke Charles made peace with Henry of Navarre because he was at the end of his resources, and received his share of 3,766,800 livres given by the King to some of the nobles who were at last "convinced" of the justice of the Béarnais' cause.

Nicole, Henry's daughter, and entered on a checkered career as Charles IV. He was rather an interesting character. There was no trace in him of the love of literature and learning and art, such as old King René had planted in many of his descendants. Latin and Greek were not this Duke's affair, but he seems to have possessed certain natural gifts, so that he did not appear ignorant on any subject. His conversation was rather inclined to buffoonery and coarse stories. His tongue ran away with him sometimes, and he had a strange fashion of mixing fact and fancy as he talked, so that no one knew what he was going to say next. His energy was untiring. Neither cold nor heat affected him, neither hunger nor thirst. He did not believe in illness. Once when his physicians tried to keep him in bed, he showed them his boots and said that they were his medicine for all ills. With that he mounted his horse and rode off.

Both his qualities and his defects excited interest because they were stamped with originality, but while he inspired curiosity, he also aroused a certain apprehension and distrust. For, with native ambition, he was tormented by a desire to astonish the world, while he never showed a real capacity for managing his own affairs. His wonderful vitality and energy did not bear fruit. Although he had been brought up in the French Court, he was more ready to affiliate with the Emperor than with Louis XIII., and almost lost his duchy by his uncertain and capricious policy in wavering between Germany and France. The Thirty Years' War brought to the fore men of precisely his type. Wallenstein and Gustavus Adolphus were the objects of his admiration, while he was no match for Richelieu when that minister pursued his consistent policy of strengthening France at the expense of the border states. When Charles made a close alliance with his kinsman, the Duke of Bavaria, Richelieu had certain archives searched at Metz and elsewhere, to prove that there were long-standing liens possessed by the bishop on some Lorraine estates, liens which had passed to the French Crown with the towns. The papers were found and justified to Richelieu's mind the *réunion* of a number of little seigniories. French authority was thus extended through the duchy.

Several times Louis XIII. marched his troops over Lorraine under one pretext or another, and the Duke was forced into signing the treaties of Vic and of Liverdun, which put the French King into possession of nearly all

Lorraine except Nancy and a few other places. Both the Duke and his duchy were hopelessly entangled in the intricacies of the Thirty Years' War. But Charles of Lorraine was not alone in his fate, nor was he the only person whose policy was shifting and uncertain in that general *mêlée*. Richelieu's comment on the Duke's cession at Liverdun (1632) was, "This is a lesson to little princes not to offend great ones unless they are ready to be ruined, and to the dukes of Lorraine that Charles Quint was quite right when he told his son [Philip II.] to 'expect nothing from them [the dukes of Lorraine], because they could not preserve their Estates without France.'"[62]

The story of his adventures and misadventures in the thirty years of conflict can not be followed. When the reckoning day came at Münster, the question of Lorraine was deferred, but the status of Metz, Toul, and Verdun was at last definitely fixed. They had not really been disturbed for nearly a century, when the Emperor formally renounced all imperial claims to the cities.

> In the same manner as they formerly belonged to the Emperor, they shall for the future appertain to the Crown of France, and shall be irrevocably incorporated therewith forever, saving the rights of the Metropolitan, which belongs to the Archbishop of Trèves.[63]

The act of cession is also perfectly explicit.[64] Whatever the rest of Lorraine might be, the towns were royal appanages. The Emperor had actually given far more than he possessed, but the cities submitted to the King as they never had to the Emperor, and the provisions were accepted. In the elapsed hundred years, the old free character of these city-states had vanished, and by the time of the Treaty of Westphalia, the article simply expressed an existing condition.

By the Treaty of the Pyrenees (1559) the Duke was nominally reinstated in his domains, but under hard conditions. He was to cede the Barrois to France and to dismantle all his Lorraine fortresses. Another treaty drawn up in February, 1661, restored Bar as a French fief, but the other towns mentioned were to be ceded and Nancy dismantled. In 1662, in a kind of desperation, he signed the Treaty of Montmartre, whereby the succession of the duchy was

---

[62] Haussonville, *Hist. de la réunion*, etc., i., p. 251.
[63] Vast, Article lxxii.
[64] *Ibid.*, p. 38.

practically sold to Louis XIV. But the Lorrainers, possibly with the secret approval of their Duke, refused to ratify this pact. He was, however, expelled from his estates and went to Germany and took part in the coalition of the Empire, Holland and Spain against France. After the French invasion of his duchy he revenged himself on the Marquis de Créqui, who had overrun Lorraine in 1670—spoiling city and country alike,—by defeating him at Conzer Brücke and receiving his capitulation at Trèves in 1675. That same year, the Duke died, having spent his life, as Voltaire said, in losing estates.

VI.

The Last Dukes of Lorraine

DURING the fifty-one years that Charles had borne his title, the French advance had been continuous, achieved both insidiously and by force of arms. The old independent, imperial status of Lorraine was practically at an end. The personal experiences of her last nominal dukes, in some respects separable from the history of the duchy, may be briefly outlined.

The heir to Charles IV. was his nephew, who at once assumed the title of Duke Charles V., and was recognized by all the Powers except France. He, too, was of an adventurous spirit. Failing of recognition as duke, he tried to secure the appointment to the throne of Poland,—just then going begging. Not succeeding in this endeavour, he engaged actively in the wars in Hungary and ended his rovings by marrying, landless prince though he was, Eleanor of Austria, sister to Emperor Leopold. When the Treaty of Nimwegen was under consideration, Louis XIV. offered to restore his estates if the heir would surrender a portion of his heritage, and submit to various curtailments of his ducal rights. These overtures were refused, and the titular duke remained in Austria until his death in 1690. His son, Leopold, was more complaisant towards the French compromises. He accepted the King's terms,—somewhat more favourable then those of 1679, but hard enough nevertheless,—consented to dismantle forts and disband garrisons, and was acknowledged Duke of Lorraine. His concessions were formulated in an article of the Peace of Ryswick (1697). French encroachments thus again received the seal of diplomatic approval, and were all accepted by the signatories to the Treaty.

Leopold's independence was under pretty effectual restraint, but he left an impress, nevertheless, upon the duchy and accomplished certain reforms. A peaceful administration was urgently needed by the land and the people. During the campaigns of Louis XIV., damage had been wrought in every direction. Deserted houses had fallen into utter ruin, titles were obscured or lost entirely, strangers had come and taken possession of property, without being questioned as to their right. In German Lorraine, a region especially open to marauders, a conglomerate of strange elements,—Swiss, Picards, Burgundians, and unknown wastrels,—had drifted in, as a result of which in many places the old speech and the old racial character were wholly altered. Leopold was quite ready to welcome immigration if it consisted of desirable human material. Indeed, he offered bonuses to settlers able to re-establish economic prosperity, but at the same time strenuous efforts were made to bar out the vagabonds bequeathed to the Rhinelands by the various armies passing through that region. It was wonderful how the country began to recuperate as soon as it was afforded a brief breathing spell. The harvests resulting from the first sowing were phenomenal. Manufactures were revived and initiated. Glass works, paper mills, porcelain factories were established at St. Dié, Lunéville, and elsewhere. Between 1699 and 1735 the population almost trebled. Besides undertaking the intelligent fostering of industry, Leopold authorized the making of a compilation of laws, known as the *Code Leopold*, which was a valuable contribution to provincial justice. Yet, in spite of identifying himself with the good of his subjects, Leopold remained a stranger in his duchy. He was essentially Germanic or at least Austrian, while the land of his ancestors had taken on a distinctively French character. It was no longer in contact with provinces of Germanic rule. It was surrounded on every side by Gallicized territory. As an imperial fief, it had become a detached waif.

When the War of the Spanish Succession broke in rudely upon the oasis of tranquillity, Leopold found himself hard pressed. The promises of neutrality given at Vienna and Paris were not respected—international ethics being still in their infancy,—and his little realm was invaded and trampled over. Leopold was forced to forsake Nancy and to set up his capital at Lunéville. There, in spite of poverty, he made his sojourn as pleasant as he could. Debt was of less concern to him than the accomplishment of his desires, and he let financial obligations pile up regardless of the future. He built a new palace, laid out a pleasure garden, constructed a theatre, and furthered elaborate entertainments in each. The participants were as care-free and gay as the courtiers of old King René, though their literary achievements were not startling. No poet seems to have gained immortality as a result of the encouragement to production. Many platitudes were spun out and the chief gift to posterity was a mountain of debt. When Leopold died in 1729, the sum had reached enormous proportions. The burden descended as a legacy to his son Francis.

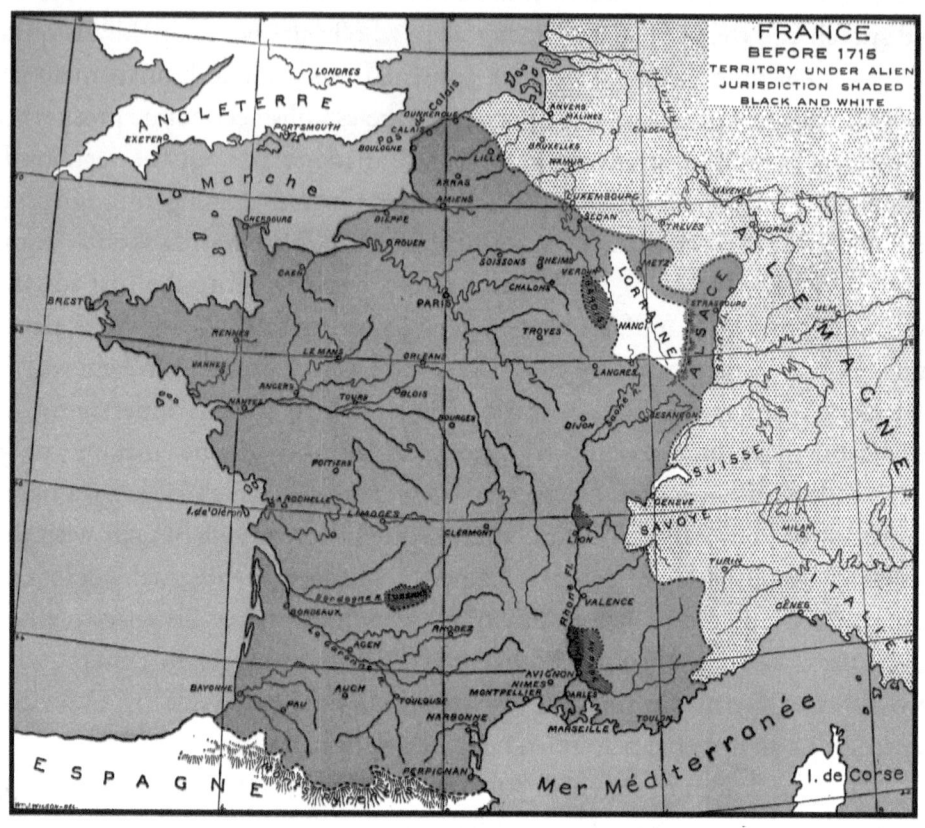

MAP NO. 7

The association of this Francis with Lorraine was brief. When he was betrothed to his cousin Maria Theresa of Habsburg, successor by Pragmatic Sanction to her father, Emperor Charles VI., Louis XV. refused to allow him to carry his duchy with him into the Empire. It was considered a reasonable prejudice on his part, for scattered fiefs were no longer counted desirable property. Accordingly, a triangular arrangement was arrived at without reference to the inhabitants whose dwelling-places were involved in the transaction. The duchy of Tuscany, just then lacking a ruler, was secured for Francis in exchange for Lorraine, which was factitiously bestowed upon the deposed King of Poland, Stanislas Leszczynski, whose daughter had married Louis XV. It was pleasant for the French monarch to provide comfortably for his father-in-law, and he rendered the provision inexpensive by arranging that on the demise of Stanislas, Lorraine should pass to his daughter, the Queen, and be incorporated into France for good. Moreover, in order to save the old man trouble, Louis XV. made a private agreement with him that the entire financial administration of Lorraine should be immediately lodged in royal hands, in return for a satisfactory pecuniary consideration paid to the titular sovereign. Then Stanislas was permitted to wear his own kingly title and keep up a stately miniature court at Lunéville. He, too, found ample time for literary amusements, relieved, as he was, by his kind son-in-law from irksome official duties.

Upon the death of Stanislas in February, 1766, the duchy of Lorraine and her allied seigniories became incorporated, *de jure* as well as *de facto*, into the realm of France.

The Duke's renunciation had been very precise.[65] Louis XV. lost no time. On the day after the death his representatives convened the Estates of the duchy and informed them that their sovereign had assumed the administration of affairs. The coat-of-arms of the Polish king was replaced by the Lilies of France, the final symbol of the political shift. In name as well as in fact, Lorraine was a French province.

---

[65] Nous déclarons, que, non obstant la répugnance que nous avons d'abandonner l'ancien patrimoine de nos pères, . . . que nous céderons et abandonnerons pareillement . . . nôtre duché de Lorraine, les appartenances et dépendances, soit d'ancien patrimoine, acquisitions ou biens allodiaux, et à quelque titre que ce puisse être, au dit Roi, beau-père de Sa Majesté très-Chrétienne et, après sa décès, à Sa Majesté . . . en tout droit de propriété et souveraineté, ainsi que nous en avons joui jusq' à présent." (Dec. 13, 1736.) *Soc. d'archéologie Lorraine*, 3e s., 1873, vol. i., p. 281.

VII.

THE FRENCH REVOLUTION

THE changes that ensued in Lorraine were not abrupt. Certain alterations in the internal organization of the duchy had already taken place during the intermittent half-French régime. More radical policies followed. For instance, the sovereign court at Nancy was reorganized into a *Parlement* for all Lorraine. Naturally the nobles protested with all their strength at the encroachments upon ancient territorial autonomy, but their strength was not great and a little later many drifted to Paris in the wake of Marie Antoinette, the daughter of their last duke, and became French courtiers. Some of them remembered their own nationality at the first outbreak of revolutionary ideas. Sufficient individuality had survived in Lorraine,—in the institutions and distinctive features that had been preserved in spite of all innovations,—to cause a revival of local-national feeling and to excite hopes of recovering all that had been cherished in the past. The *cahier* that was presented on behalf of Lorraine to the National Assembly of 1789 contained a long list of demands which, later, the Assembly made its own. The list comprised the following items: regular convention of provincial Estates, self-taxation, equal assessment on all, abolition of privilege, personal security, abolition of *lettres de cachet*, freedom of the press, admission of the Third Estate to all offices, reform in justice and education, freedom in industry and communication, abolition of internal taxation, etc.[66] There were live minds in Lorraine and pens capable of expressing thoughts.

In the duchy, as in Alsace, there persisted quite a large number of small estates and fiefs retaining feudal relations with the Empire. Regulation of the precise status of these had been postponed from time to time and many points were still unsettled when the great crisis occurred. In the end these holdings were treated as was the property of the *émigrés*. On February 14th, 1793, they were incorporated into the Republic. The territory once known as the duchies of Lorraine and of Bar and the Three Sees were redivided into the

---

[66] Derichsweiler, *Geschichte Lothringens*, ii., p. 623.

Departments of the Meurthe, of the Meuse, the Vosges, and the Moselle, the last named embracing German Lorraine and the *Pays messin*.

In Lorraine, as in Alsace, there was immense enthusiasm for the Revolution and confidence in the New France. Perhaps a greater admiration for Napoleon prevailed in the land that had been distinguished for its militarism and its chivalrous nobility than in Alsace, where democratic theories aroused a greater measure of zealous devotion to the France of which the Alsatians were proud to feel themselves a part. Mulhouse, long attached to Switzerland as a tiny, self-sustaining statelet, went over joyously to the greater Republic on the wave of a popular vote and was not sorry to abide by the decision of the plebiscite when Napoleon was winning laurels for the nation chosen.

In military skill and in religious zeal, Lorraine was true to her old traditions during the epoch of the Napoleonic wars. Among the great French generals native to her soil were Ney, Oudinot, Victor, St. Cyr, Gerard, Lobau, Kellermann, Munier, Mouton, Regnier, and others, while a large number of devoted sisters of charity, as well as the host of common soldiers, won golden reputations. They held loyally to Napoleon to the very last.

> At the Congress of Vienna (1814–15), the political fate of Lorraine hung in the balance during the diplomatic deliberations; there seem to have been various informal suggestions as to her disposition. Austria was inclined to think that the arrangement with Louis XIV. had served its purpose and that the lands annexed by him could be as easily released. There was some talk to the effect that the left bank of the Rhine was essentially German, but nothing came of it. There was much for the statesmen to settle. Metternich said that Prussia was like a garter, she required substance to enclose. They wanted her "fat, but not too fat," and were willing to sacrifice Saxony or Poland to attain just the proportions that would give her weight without pulling down the scales.[67] The talk about the "number of souls" that could be deducted from

---

[67] At the beginning of the Bavarian war in 1778, the following sentiments were expressed by the Emperor of Austria and his minister. "Of the Netherlands, which might be called, geographically, the head of Austria, alas, the long neck, Lorraine, was once ours, but whose is it? Irrecoverable for the present but perhaps may not always be so." "Make the Reich a reality again, make Austria great; Austria *is* the Reich. How else can the Reich be real?"

These phrases were perfectly true of the Austria of that period. But in 1814, her statesmen were apparently far more preoccupied with Prussia and her ambitions than with Austria's own demands. At least that is the impression gained from Metternich.

Saxony for Prussia's benefit shows how this supreme effort in behalf of legitimacy used methods that do not seem very legitimate.[68] Some strips of territory belonging to Lorraine and to Alsace too, were juggled about for divers reasons; for example, Landau, one of the cities of the Alsatian Decapole, fell to Rhenish Prussia, but the main portion remained to France. The Congress finished its labours, slightly complicated by Napoleon's little journey from Elba, and Europe settled down for a period of peace.

---

[68] "In the project for reconstitution sent by Prussia to the Conference on January 19th, she still demanded the whole of Saxony; declared at the same time that with the countries which she claimed on the Rhine she would have 680,000 more subjects than at the epoch of her greatest splendour. But this scheme did not alarm anyone; as it was certain that Prussia could be brought down very much in her demands."

"Prussia was offered 800,000 subjects in Saxony and 1,400,000 on the Rhine. Her population was thus increased to above 10,000,000 souls."

Memoir by Frederick von Gentz, Feb. 12, 1815.
Memoirs of Prince Metternich, ii., pp. 572–3.

VIII.

The Language

AS a French province, or rather as four French departments, how large a German element did the ducal territory contain during the nineteenth century? That is a hard question to settle and contradictory statements meet one at every turn. Metz, Gallo-Roman in early periods, seems to have contained a preponderance of the French long before her annexation to France. In a list of 115 magistrates of the twelfth century there appear only three names that are evidently German—Rinck, Desch, and Hanque. Later, down to the fifteenth century, both magistrates and officials bear ordinary French names. In many remote regions, however, such a preponderance did not obtain. As he travelled across the Alps, Duke Anthony was very much astonished to meet some merchants from Valdevanges belonging to his duchy, who spoke a dialect compounded of Romance and German. This occurred in the fifteenth century. Anthony had spent so much of his life at the French court that he did not know his peoples' customs.

Then there were other waves of usage and of linguistic regulations. When Stanislas was playing his rather absurd part as Duke of Lorraine, he issued the following edict:

> Part of our duchy of Lorraine known under the name of *German*, being near to Alsace and the Empire, . . . it happens that many of our subjects, living in that region, for the sake of convenience, have totally abandoned the use of French, which is, however, the national language of the people of our duchy; and although, following the example of our predecessors, we have taken the precaution of confiding judicial and notarial offices only to men familiar with both languages, French and German, for the administering of justice and with instructions to draw up instruments in the first of these languages, we are, nevertheless, informed that many of them use German in writing the sentences, judgments, acts, contracts, and procedures which they draft on the subject of the affairs and of the litigation of the said inhabitants, concerning property and commerce. This encourages them [the clients] to abandon their native tongue for one that is foreign to them; and desiring to check the

progress of an abuse so contrary to a uniformity of ideas necessary among the subjects of one sovereignty and at the same time so prejudicial to the weal of our service—etc.[69]

This attempt to check a bilingual tendency by legislation seems to show that it prevailed only sectionally and was not universal in any very wide region. Undoubtedly the German spoken—when it was not the Lorraine patois—was a debased speech, French being the standard for the better classes. It does not seem, from casual observation, that the knowledge of German was very extensive, although Frederick the Great assumes that a "Lorrainer" ought to understand German.

We have, however, the testimony of Edmond About that even the Alsatians,—whose patois was undoubtedly German,—could not understand high German easily. He tells the story that in 1871 the people of Saverne (Zabern) were persuaded to send a petition to Bismarck declaring their submission, hoping in that way to retain a tribunal in their town. A little advocate drew up the paper and a certain old archæologist, Dagobert Fischer, translated it into German. Anxious to show those in Berlin that some Alsatians, at least, were proficient in German the old man elaborated the phrases into three pages of difficult handwriting. The people were told that they had better submit to necessity and that by signing they would save their town. No one could read the text—no one knew that in signing he was subscribing to the declaration that "Our origin, our customs, our hearts are German." The petition was carried from house to house until a workman, who knew German, refused to sign until he had mastered the contents of the paper destined for the German Chancellor. "But it is an infamy," he cried, and so thought the signers when he explained matters. There was a rush to revoke signatures. Too late—the advocate had hurriedly completed his work and the petition was on its way to Berlin on a night train. The desired tribunal was retained in the town, but Saverne was not happy in her success.

Thus when 1871 brought about the separation of the territory from France, no true linguistic affinity appears to soften the annexation to Germany.

---

[69] Godron, p. 320.

ELSASS-LOTHRINGEN

THE territory formally ceded to Germany at Frankfort (May, 1871) was incorporated into the German Empire as a *Reichsland*,—an Imperial Land,—under the designation, Elsass-Lothringen. This did not mean, however, that the whole of the sometime French provinces were transferred to Germany. The newly created unit consisted of the major part of Alsace and about one-fifth of Lorraine, as can be seen by Map 8. It comprised the departments of Haut-Rhin and Bas Rhin, exclusive of Belfort and a small tract of country, together with the department of the Moselle and portions of the departments of the Meurthe and the Vosges. The ceded portion of Lorraine, covered by the department names, consisted of the so-called German Lorraine and Metz with the *Pays messin*,—the district surrounding the city. This entire *Reichsland* has an area of 5601 square miles. The maximum length is 145 miles, N. to S., the maximum breadth E. to W. 105 miles, the minimum breadth 24 miles. It is bounded S. by Switzerland, E. by the Rhine,—Baden lies on the opposite bank of the river,—N.E. and E. by the Bavarian Palatinate, Rhenish Prussia, and Luxemburg, W. by France. The surface is varied, consisting of mountain, plateau, and plain land, thus giving opportunity for pastoral, grazing, agricultural, pomocultural, and forest occupations. The climate is temperate, rather moist, owing to the many streams, and with certain variations because of the various altitudes, and because snow lies on the summits of the Vosges Mountains for about half the year. Potatoes, cereals, sugar-beets, hops, tobacco, flax, and hemp are among the valuable products, but the greatest profit comes from grapes and fruit for which the uplands of Alsace are peculiarly advantageous. The plains of Lorraine are less fertile than the soil of Alsace, but are rich in coal, iron, and salt mines. The recent discovery of a new process by which detrimental phosphorus could be eliminated from the iron ore gave a great stimulus to the iron industry in all its phases.

As it was in Roman times so today, there is more commerce in Alsace. Her cities, lying on the great railways between north and south as they did on the ancient highways, are natural trade centres for a radius of territory. During the last few years manufacture has increased notably, textiles, glass, and many other wares being produced in the factories. The greatest output is in cotton cloth, Mülhausen, Colmar, and certain Vosges towns being the centres of the industry.

In 1903, the population numbered 1,874,014. Of these, over a million are Catholics, 32,379 Jews, and the remainder, Protestants. The native speech of the majority is Germanic, as the last Census gives 250,000 as the official number of French-speaking people.

I.

After the Cession

IN 1871, France found herself in a difficult position. A war, begun by the Emperor Napoleon III. against Prussia, aided by the remaining German states as confederated friends and allies, was concluded by the new French Republic under pressure of difficulties within as well as without. Statesmen had to handle unknown conditions thrust upon them by the fall of the Napoleonic régime and to calm the discontent of the radical spirits of France, delighted to be free of the shackles of the Third Empire but very unwilling to accept the limitations of a conservative administration—an administration which was practically forced into compromises. And puzzled, half-shattered France found that the other party to the desired, nay, necessary peace was no longer Prussia, backed up strongly, but a German Empire formed at Versailles itself. It was evident that French soil could not be cleared without sacrifices of land, of money, and of dignity. There were terrible heartburnings. The final treaty signed at Frankfort, May 10, 1871, "brought the major part of Alsace, together with the eastern piece of German Lorraine, . . . back to the newly founded German Empire." That a *newly founded* institution could receive *back* territory it was too young to have lost, sounds a trifle illogical, but such is the concrete statement made by the scholarly German historian in the concluding pages of his history of Lorraine.[70] By decree of July 9, 1871, the Westmark was incorporated into the German Empire "forever," the same term of occupation that had been allotted to the same land in title-deeds represented by the list of treaties already mentioned. With every new clash of arms, the scraps of paper had been rewritten and all had contained the same pledge of perpetuity that was now repeated to the advantage of the freshly inaugurated body politic. Elsass-Lothringen, as the ceded section was to be called henceforth, was not annexed to Prussia, as the Rhinelands had been in earlier pacts. It was simply incorporated into the new State as a Reichsland. As an accession it was *Kaiserliches*, not *Kaiserliches-Koenigliches*. Kingdoms, grand-duchies,

---

[70] Derichsweiler, *Geschichte Lothringens*, ii., p. 627.

duchies, principalities, three free towns,—all retained some autonomy when they became integral parts of the Imperial federation, but the Reichsland, won by their united efforts in military action, was Imperial property in which, nominally, at least, all the states had an interest.

The regulations for the administration of the artificially created unit were enacted at first as those of a provisional government. The whole was divided into three districts,—Upper and Lower Alsace and Lorraine, and these districts were again divided into circles. At the head of the administration was an Upper President, with powers almost dictatorial,—his official residence being Strasburg. Two years later, January, 1874, the German imperial constitution was substituted for this interim government. Writs were issued for the election of fifteen deputies to the Imperial Diet and in the same year an Elsass—Lothringen committee was instituted. At first the sessions of this body were not open, but later its scope was enlarged and its nature changed. Its acts all had to be approved, however, by the Federal Council (*Bundesrat*). A council (*Oberpraesidium*) for the province was in vogue after July 4, 1879. The supreme official was a governor (*Statthalter*) whose seat was Strasburg. To him were given the powers of the Upper President and to him the Kaiser deputed an executive authority, subject to veto. A ministry assumed responsibility for all governmental transactions and could also veto the governor's acts. In the Federal Council (*Bundesrat*), which is the source of legislative power for the Empire, and to which were submitted the accounts of the public house-keeping, the governor had a vote. The governor or viceroy was assisted by four ministers of departments under the presidency of a secretary of state, and, when occasion required it, by a council of state (*Staatsrat*) consisting of the secretary of state, under-secretaries, the president of the supreme court of the territory, and, as a rule, by twelve nominees of the emperor. The parliamentary committee (*Landesausschuss*[71]) consisted of 58 members, 34 appointed by district councils (*Bezirkstäge*), 4 by the large towns, and 20 by the rural districts. Two commissioners represented Elsass-Lothringen in the Federal Council but had no vote.

It must not be thought for a minute that cession, reconstruction, and German-directed administration were accepted smoothly and resignedly.

---

[71] This term is used even in French. It was a peculiar body with no real legislative power.

There were bitter protests from the inhabitants against any forcible transference of their homes, their communities, their institutions, to another nationality. A passionate petition was sent to Bordeaux where the statesmen of the Third Republic were at their work of reorganization. To a man like Edmond About, born in Lorraine, resident in Alsace because he loved its quaint individuality, the cession seemed simply inconceivable. He wandered from place to place, despairingly, during his first visit after the war.

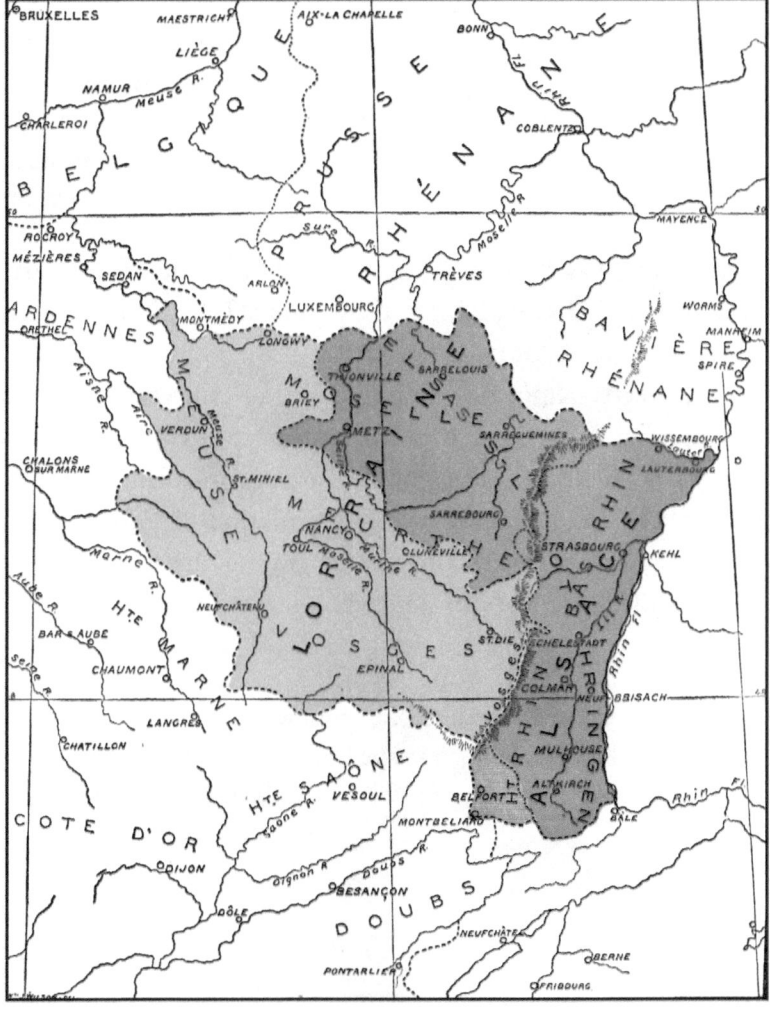

MAP NO. 8

Territory Annexed by Germany, 1817. Parts of Lorraine and of Alsace Retained by France.

Prince Bismarck seems to have had a certain prevision of the disadvantages which the proposed annexation might entail. In the beginning of the Franco-Prussian War he considered certain possibilities. The uniting of Alsace and Metz to Baden as a Reichsland seemed to him a desirable measure to ensure a strong little state that might be an available unit in the consolidated confederation that was to have only one mind, but which might find a small voice helpful in reaching unanimity. He is quoted as saying to the Mayor of Versailles:

> Germany wants peace and will make war until she gets it, let the consequences be ever so lamentable from a humane point of view. . . . This peace will be secured by a line of fortresses between Strasburg and Metz, as well as by those two towns which will protect Germany against the dread of a second attack by France.

This declaration was made on October 7, 1870.[72] The preliminary articles of peace were signed February 26, 1871, by Thiers, Jules Favre, and Bismarck. By that time the Chancellor had gone far from the opinion he had expressed in 1867 to Mr. Beatty-Kingston, "Suppose France entirely conquered, and a Prussian garrison in Paris; what are we to do with our victory? We could not even decently take Alsace, for the Alsatians are become Frenchmen and wish to remain so."[73] The morning after the capitulation of Paris, Bismarck saw reason to change his mind respecting Alsace, but he differentiated between it and Lorraine according to the same journalist's report of his words to the same journalist:

> As you see, we are keeping Metz; but I confess I do not like that part of the arrangement. Strasburg is German in speech, and will be so in heart ten years hence. Metz, however, is French, and will be a hotbed of disaffection for a long time to come.[74]

---

[72] *Conversations with Prince Bismarck*, collected by Heinrich von Poschinger, tr. by Sidney Whitman, p. 25. See also Dipl. Circular in Anderson's Constitutions, etc., France, p. 599.

[73] *Conversations*, p. 86.

[74] *Ibid.*, p. 98.

BELFORT IN ALSACE AFTER ANNEXATION TO FRANCE, 1674
From a reproduction of a sketch in *Mémoires de deux voyages et séjours en Alsace, 1674–76 and 1681.*
(H. De l'Hermine)

It is possible that the Englishman did not know of the emphatic utterance made to the mayor in October. Or it may be that Bismarck really saw the matter under different aspects from time to time as he penetrated into French conditions.

The discussions about the details of the final adjustment were protracted and filled with a succession of humiliating incidents for the conquered French. The indemnity demanded was enormous, and Thiers tried his hardest to secure better terms. He was determined to retain the two cities, Belfort in Alsace and Metz in Lorraine, from the territorial cession. Metz was refused. In regard to Belfort, Bismarck consulted the King and returned to Thiers with this answer: "In pursuance of the King's desire, I have had to demand the entry of our troops into Paris. . . . You have . . . requested that this clause be omitted. We will concede this if you will leave us Belfort." This offer was refused with some indignation. Paris could not sell Belfort to escape an indignity. After more discussion Thiers gained his point and Belfort remained in the possession of France. This arrangement was arrived at in Versailles[75] on February 23d.

In May the discussions were resumed at Frankfort, preceding the signing of the treaty as finally worded. The French negotiators attempted to obtain an extension of the territory around Belfort. Bismarck promised to investigate the point in question and suggested that the extension might be granted in return for concessions elsewhere. The Frenchmen protested against this suggestion as they were not empowered to dispose of territory unspecified in their instructions. Nevertheless, on the following day, May 8th, Bismarck announced that he agreed to the Belfort extension but wished in compensation therefor a strip about ten kilometres in extent along the Luxemburg frontier. The French would thus obtain 27,000 inhabitants and 6,000 hectares on the upper Rhine while losing 7,000 inhabitants and 10,000 hectares.[76] The matter had to be referred to the Chamber of Deputies, which finally decided upon what should be done.

---

[75] *Conversations*, p. 52.

[76] *Conversations*, p. 67. The author adds: "The German Cabinet was induced to make this proposal for two important reasons: the one to obtain the rich iron-ore deposits of the locality in question; the other, to diminish the French frontier towards Luxemburg by one-third. The Chancellor also mentioned a third reason, of minor importance from the point of view of

From the reports of Bismarck's attitude towards the land-transfer, one fact emerges. His motives for demanding the readjustment of territory were not based on the constitution of the Roman Empire or of the old German Kingdom but on his conviction that the new Germany must be adequately guarded from the west. He seems to have appraised, justly, the then existing relations between France and Alsace, and to have decided to disregard obvious disadvantages for the sake of what he considered of greater importance. Years after, he declared that no foot of the annexed land could be safely returned, but he seems to have regarded the annexation itself as an act of *force majeure* amply justified by the attending circumstances.

In the minds of other Germans, however, there was, a firm, deep-seated belief that wanderers had simply returned to the fold. There was a persistent inclination to count the *Deutsches Reich*, created in 1871, not as the offspring of the North German Confederation, but as the heir in fee to the Holy Roman Empire, laid to rest in 1806. It was as though a vigorous, able-bodied, intelligent young phoenix lovingly cherished a few ashes it found on the ground, instead of realizing that it could never have come to life had it not been for the political artists who gave it actual existence from more substantial elements than the remnants of a burnt-out fire. Some feathers used belonged more rightfully to Austria, it would seem, than to Prussia. Certainly this remark applies in so far as Alsace and Lorraine were concerned. As a matter of fact, the Prussian-headed empire had no need of any refurbished insignia to establish its prestige. It quickly proved its ability to win its own laurels and to found and build up a solid nation such as had not had foot-hold in Germany during any epoch of the past. But, singularly enough, even such an authoritative historian as Heinrich von Sybel, with wide experience as a statesman, prefers the shadowy claim to the simple assertion that a territory had been gained by right of conquest, while its old title-deeds in treaty articles were just as valid as its new. In his brief for Germany's right to the acquired provinces, he proves, to his satisfaction, the point of ancient possession, but

---

positive policy, for the territory which Prussia desired to possess had been the scene of repeated and bloody struggles. The mortal remains of a large number of officers and soldiers were there laid to rest, and the Emperor attached importance to the possession of their graves."

he has some sympathy for the battered human occupants of the lands.[77] In conclusion, he says:

> We know, indeed, that the Lorrainers, since 1766, the Alsatians, since 1801, have become good Frenchmen, and to-day, oppose, by a large majority, the reunion with their Fatherland. For such an attitude, we do not deny, we feel respect. The inhabitants were born and brought up in the great French commonwealth; they would be men destitute of common feeling and patriotism if, notwithstanding their German speech, they did not consider themselves French to-day. But we trust to the power of Nature; water can be diverted for a time into artificial channels, but with the removal of the dam will flow with the full stream. If to-day the inhabitants find the French more sympathetic than the Germans, soon they will find themselves among their own kind in Germany. In Germany they will find the best gifts of the French State, the consciousness and security of a mighty commonwealth, a sound harvest of science and art, a wide market for their industry and a progressive parliamentary life. They will have lighter taxes, greater religious freedom, numerous schools, and in the army will meet the sons of the educated classes.

Another writer, Derichsweiler, already cited, says that the joy in Germany over the "recovery" of the long-lost lands was intense. It is worth while glancing at the substance of some passages as expressed in his rather flowery periods, because his fervent sentiments really seem to echo certain ideas of New Germany.[78] It was thought, he says, that the province would be like an ancient parchment, whose original text had been covered by a new script, yet not so much destroyed that it could not be restored to legibility by a skilful hand. A discerning eye could detect in the Westmark the sub-structure of pristine customs, civilization, and racial unity, evidences of a background essentially Germanic, just visible through the obscuring foreign tissue spread over it. Both statesmen and laymen welcomed this simile as an illuminating suggestion. If, in essentials, the people of the Reichsland were just as German as they were when Abbe von Gorse lamented that his fellow-Lorrainers would insist on copying decadent fashions from the French, the only requirement

---

[77] "Deutschlands Rechte auf Elsass und Lothringen," *Kleine Historische Schriften*, Heinrich von Sybel, iii., p. 457, Stuttgart, 1880.

[78] *Geschichte Lothringens*, ii., p. 630 *et seq.*

was to rub off the whitewash, as from a concealed decoration, and the inherent German spirit would be revealed in all its beauty and integrity.

This confident belief held at first, that an *"undeutsche Grundschrift"*—a non-German script—lay no deeper than the surface, was, however, doomed to bitter disappointment. After two decades of German occupation it became evident that the souls of the Alsatians and Lorrainers, when they "returned to the German Empire, were not, to use the phrase of a certain author, foreign-glazed German crystals." They had suffered a terminal if not a sea change. A "transsubstantiation" had taken place. In many respects it was the outer form that had remained German, while the soul itself had altered. A French spirit had honeycombed the old nationality and over-mastered it in thought, ideas, and sentiment, in the general attitude towards life, in the mental conception of life's true worth. This change had been brought about imperceptibly because the Westmark had passed over to France piecemeal. Lorraine, Strasburg, Schlestadt were destitute of German national sentiment. Their first real nationality had come from the New France. What knew they of New Germany? During their absence in France,

> a spring-spirit, such as the world had never before experienced, had breathed over the desolate intellectual wastes and kissed into life a rich harvest of thought from which the noblest elements of the "Ausland" have drawn their nourishment. Under the lead of divinely endowed men, the German nation has been re-built on a new plan.

This is what the man of the Westmark was ignorant of in 1871:

> He knew nothing of our renaissance. So he returned, a Gallicized stranger, to an Empire grown strange in its new intellectual splendour. Only a wretched fragment of German speech remained to him, and this fragment was wholly insufficient for intellectual purposes. The only intellectual life he knew moved to French rhythm. To France, Alsatians and Lorrainers had looked for cultivation, and to Germany they were alien.

They had not attained the best that France could give her own children and they had lost all German idealism. They were strange hybrids. Their greatest loss was that "half-mystic" feeling for nature characteristic of young Germany. They did not possess that dreamy ideality (*träumerische Idealität*), etc.

The words are perfervid and the metaphors rather mixed, but the author's meaning finds expression. It was generally anticipated in Germany that the annexed lands would be quickly nationalized. That anticipation had not been realized in 1901, after a lapse of thirty years. If one may trust a writer[79] in *Le Correspondant*, November 10, 1914, that nationalization has still not been achieved. The exertions of the imperial government have not succeeded in wooing to contentment the people of the Reichsland.

Undoubtedly it was a difficult population with which to deal. Edmond About states that out of 1,100,000 Alsatians, 600,000 refused to accept German nationality, and took their way across the border westward, or farther westward across the sea. The number of migrating Lorrainers is put at 45,000,—more in proportion as the ceded territory was much smaller. Those who felt strongly and were in a position to go, left their land to fellow-countrymen, less intense in feeling and less capable of action.

The figure of 600,000 probably overstates, and the official number of 270,000 understates, the extent of emigration. The latter is the sum of the "optants" who registered their choice of nationality on the appointed days in October, 1872. But the first general exodus was followed by more departures as the years went on and German military service became imminent for sons of the family. There were some strange cases of change of base where sentiment was the sole bond between the *émigrés* and their new environment. In Elboef, Normandy, there is a Lutheran congregation for whom an Alsatian pastor officiates in German once a fortnight. After the service there is much friendly conversation in the old patois of Bischwiller, an Alsatian town, five hundred kilometres away from the Norman church. It was a town once belonging to the Bishop of Strasburg (*Bischoviswiler, Episcopi villa*), and contained 11,500 inhabitants in 1869. In 1874, there were 7700, and many of the German-speaking Lutheran weavers, had found their way to Normandy where the work to which they were accustomed was to be had—national feeling alone outweighing other considerations of language and creed.

In Alsace, immigration from Germany soon set in to offset the losses in population, and the proportion between indigenous Alsatians and immigrants again becomes difficult to appraise. There has been little desire to

---

[79] Chanoine Collin—"En Lorraine—La Protestation et la Germanisation."

forget the differences and to form one society, although, perhaps, the gulf is not so great as represented in the romantic literature dealing with Alsace. Still, the newcomers from Baden and elsewhere across the Rhine were not welcomed any more heartily than the Suevians were in 57 B.C. Centuries after that episode, when the immigrants from Swabia certainly formed a settled part of the population, the name lingered as designating an undesirable. "*Quia Alsatiæ hodie Suevones esse dici nolunt*"—"The Alsatians do not like to be called Suevones"—is the testimony given by the Jesuit father, Koenig, of Fribourg, in the seventeenth century. The Latin word has a dignified sound, but there is other evidence to show that the vernacular, less elegant than *Suevonis*, was used as an opprobrious term on the streets of Strasburg, and the epithet of "Schwob" lingered, to be repeated to the disadvantage of many worthy "Old Germans" as the new settlers are called.[80]

Industrial workers have not, probably, found the gulf between themselves and the native proletariat as unsurpassable as it is pictured as being between the higher classes of the social scale, especially as the educational influence exerted upon the children in the schools, from the lowest grade up, has been systematically in favour of Germany. And, in the upper classes, too, after forty years, there must be many of the younger generation, educated at home, who find the new order not unbearable. The University of Strasburg was reorganized under the name of *Kaiser Wilhelm's Universität*, and the faculty was reinforced by able German professors whose influence cannot have been without effect, even though the old Alsatian spirit is nourished by such ceremonies as the annual midnight procession, in perfect silence, around the statue of Kleber.

The demand for a change in the political government from the complete dependence on Berlin was at last met by the granting of a constitution by the

---

[80] During the past eighteen months there have been a great number of articles on Alsace and Lorraine in the periodical literature of various nations. Even Germans, who would not admit that there was a "question" to be discussed, have given some consideration to various historical points. In an interesting and sympathetic paper entitled "Alsace-Lorraine—a Study in Conquest" (*Atlantic Monthly*, May, 1914), Dr. David Starr Jordan has covered the ground of the various theories and suggestions afloat up to this year in their regard. From Italy comes the voice of Professor Ferrero. These last, the American and the Italian, agree that the land will be content with nothing but home rule *within* the German Empire. But this was early in 1914.

Reichstag on May 16, 1911. It was put into effect the following year. The articles did not embody the desires of the people themselves, as they were drafted at Berlin and were not sub mitted to the approval of the Reichsland. The inhabitants were not changed from their status of being part of the Imperial possessions without autonomy,—as being "Germans of the second class." But an advance was made towards the desired status, and there was an evident effort on the part of the framers of the constitution to secure representation of the various sections of the population.

The *Statthalter* is still appointed by the Emperor as his representative, but the *Landesausschuss* was replaced by a bi-cameral *Landtag* or parliament, with a certain degree of legislative power.

The Upper House consists of three classes of members:

I. 1. The bishops of Strasburg and Metz. During a vacancy in either See, one of the older episcopal coadjutors may be a substitute for the bishop.

2. The President of the Upper Consistory of the churches of the Augsburg Confession.

3. The President of the Synod of the Reformed Church—more exactly, the President of the Synodal Committee of the Reformed Church.

4. The President of the *Oberlandesgericht* at Colmar. (This corresponds generally, though not precisely with, the chief justice of a state supreme court.)

II. 1. A representative of the Kaiser Wilhelm's University of Strasburg elected by the whole University from the full professors, *i.e.*, those entitled to give lectures and to hold University offices.

2. One representative of the Hebrew Consistory elected by that body from among their members.

3. One representative of the cities of Strasburg, Metz, Colmar, and Mülhausen, elected by the Common Councils of these cities from their number.

4. One representative of the Chamber of Commerce elected by the Chambers of those same four cities.

5. Two representatives elected by the Commission of Agriculture from farmers by profession in the Districts of Upper and Lower Alsace and Lorraine. One of these must be a peasant proprietor of one of the districts.

6. Two representatives elected by the Industrial Guilds (*Handwerkskammer*) at Strasburg.

III. Appointees by the Kaiser on the nomination of the Bundesrat. These must be members of the Empire, resident in Elsass-Lothringen. The number of members of this class cannot exceed the number of representatives. There are forty-one members in the Chamber (1913).

The Second Chamber consists of 60 deputies elected for five years by male suffrage.[81]

In the opinion of some writers, if this constitution had been in vogue thirty years earlier instead of the semi-military administration that had held sway, it would have been an efficient instrument. So far it does not seem to have afforded satisfaction, because it falls short of placing the province in the grade it desires in comparison with the twenty-five other states in the Empire. But the shortcomings of the constitution are not, apparently, the chief ground for such dissatisfaction as continued to exist in Elsass-Lothringen. There were several minor elements of irritation, pin-pricks (*coups d'épingle*) of annoyance that did more to disturb harmony than larger political grievances. Among these, the chief were the "laws of exception" (*lois d'exception—Abwehrgesetze*) and the regulations about the use of French. The first permitted arbitrary acts and the second interfered with habits of speech that had always been current. One German writer remarks in relation to the cession of Alsace, that it was very trying to hear words distorted from their primal German form. "Wagner masqueraded as Vagneur," etc. As it is equally trying to see Kales for Calais, Nanzig, for Nancy, etc., it is perfectly comprehensible that any arbitrary system which forcibly transfers a familiar name from one language form to another would make the world seem out of tune.

It is hard to see what political affiliation would really suit the border lands now, after drifting and straining at their ropes while firmly anchored. In 1913, autonomy within the Empire was what the residents thought of, in spite of the ardent aspirations of the *émigrés* who loved to hang wreaths on the statue of Strasburg in Paris. Edmond About desired to see a small neutral state formed to fill in the gap between Switzerland and Luxemburg, so that France and Germany would not come in direct touch with each other and thus be mutually protected from invasion. But About believed in neutrality!

---

[81] *Kuerschners Staatshandbuch*, 1913, Muenchen.

Something of their very own both Alsace and Lorraine certainly want. The cries still seem to be in both quarters:

> "Français ne peux,
> Prussien ne veux,
> Alsacien suis."

> "Vous avez pu germaniser la plaine
> Mais nôtre cœur, vous ne l'aurez jamais."

APPENDIX

I.

THE TREATIES

DIPLOMATIC ARTICLES BY WHICH THE POLITICAL STATUS OF ALSACE AND LORRAINE, IN THEIR ENTIRETY OR IN PARTS, HAS BEEN AFFECTED. THERE ARE, IN ADDITION, A NUMBER OF PRIVATE COMPACTS, ESPECIALLY AS REGARDS LORRAINE.

Treaty of Verdun, 843. By division of the Frankish Empire between the grandsons of Charles the Great, territory including Alsace and Lorraine was allotted to Emperor Lothaire, the eldest brother. It was thus comprised in the Middle Kingdom.

Treaty of Meersen, 870. Charles the Bald and Louis the German divided the realm of Lothaire, except Italy, between them. In a way the divisions of Europe into France and Germany were indicated. Alsace fell to the share of Louis the German king. Lorraine was not well defined in the partition. Neither of the brothers was Emperor.

Treaty of St. Omer, 1469. Sigismund of Austria mortgaged his possessions in Upper Alsace to Charles of Burgundy. The lands were delivered to the jurisdiction of Charles.

Treaty of Nancy, 1473. Charles of Burgundy became "protector" of Lorraine by convention with Yolande of Vaudemont and René II. of Lorraine. The terms were very favourable to Charles.

Treaty of Cateau-Cambresis, 1559. This treaty settled matters after seven years of hostilities, begun by Emperor Charles V. and Henry II. of France, and concluded after Philip II. and Ferdinand had succeeded, as King and Emperor, and divided the dignities worn by Charles. This division probably made a difference in the acceptation of terms. Philip had little interest in Metz, Toul, and Verdun, imperial cities taken by the French King, and did not object to their remaining under French sovereignty. They were not specified in the treaty but simply stayed in French possession by default. Toul and Verdun have been continuously French since 1559, while Metz was French until 1871. This was the first entry of France into Lorraine.

At that time France also gained possession of Calais. These four cities were her chief asset at that time. She was forced to relinquish much more territory that she had acquired during the war.

Treaty of Westphalia, 1648. Certain rights in Alsace were ceded to Louis XIV. in accordance with Articles lxxv., lxxvi., lxxix., lxxxix., by the Emperor and the Archduke of Austria. France thereby obtained a foothold in Alsace.

The provisions were ambiguous as to the degree of power actually acquired by France. Louis XIV. was slow to claim as much as he ultimately obtained on the strength of these same provisions.

Article vi. provided for a later settlement of the controversy touching Lorraine.

Article lxxii. confirmed France in the possession of Metz; Toul, and Verdun.

Treaty of the Pyrenees, 1659. Article lxi. recorded approval of the King of Spain, as member of the House of Habsburg, to the cession in Alsace. Articles lxii.–lxxviii. refer to the relations between the Duke of Lorraine and Louis XIV.

Capitulation of Strasburg, 1681. Strasburg was unable to defend herself or to get aid from the Empire when Louis XIV. demanded her surrender. There was no resistance, practically. Articles of submission were signed on September 30, 1681.

Treaty of Nimwegen, 1679. Ten articles—xii. to xxii.—specified the terms on which Louis XIV. agreed to recognize Charles V. as Duke of Lorraine. The terms were very humiliating and the Duke preferred to remain in exile in Austria rather than accept his hereditary duchy in complete subordination to the French King. After his death, in 1690, his son accepted a compromise.

The articles of the Treaty of Westphalia were confirmed in such a manner as to give Louis XIV. the pretext of interpreting the former to his liking and of proceeding to incorporate into France the ten Alsatian cities, claiming independence and immediacy to the Empire. The *Chambres de réunions* were formed to annex these cities one after the other, as a result of the Treaty of Nimwegen.

Treaty of Ryswick, 1697. Article xvi. confirmed Louis XIV. unequivocally in his possession of Strasburg and of the major portion of Alsace. Certain estates on Alsatian territory remained in the possession of German nobles who sat in the Diet. Alsace was practically French from this date, but there were localities excepted from French jurisdiction.

Fifteen articles—xxviii. to xliii.—were devoted to the terms on which Leopold, son of Charles V. of Lorraine, was reinstated in his hereditary duchy, which had been held by the French King since 1670. The terms were hard but somewhat less so than those of the Treaty of Nimwegen. Nancy, for instance, was not retained by the French, but the forts were dismantled, and real ducal sovereignty curtailed very nearly to the point of extinction.

Treaty of Vienna, 1738. This treaty confirmed what had been agreed upon in a preliminary paper of 1736. Francis, Duke of Lorraine, ceded his duchy and appurtenances to Louis XV. forever. The Duke received the duchy of Tuscany in compensation. The reason of the cession was that Francis had married Maria Theresa, acknowledged by Pragmatic Sanction as the successor to her father, Emperor of Austria. Thus the House of Lorraine entered into the heritage of the Habsburgs and there it has remained.

Stanislas, ex-King of Poland, became titular Duke of Lorraine for his lifetime. In 1766, by virtue of this treaty, Lorraine was merged in the French realm.

Treaty of Lunéville, 1801. France was confirmed in possession of Alsace.

Act of the Assembly of France, 1795. An act abolishing all feudal conditions aroused the protests of the German Alsatian nobles against the destruction of their property rights. The Judicial Committee urged that the union of Alsace to France should be referred to the Alsatians.

The property of the Imperial nobles was treated on a par with that of the *émigrés*.

1798. The free city of Mulhouse, associated with Switzerland, but independent, voluntarily joined the French Republic after a popular vote of the inhabitants.

Congress of Vienna, 1815. France was confirmed in possession of both Alsace and Lorraine.

Treaty of Frankfort, 1871. Articles i.–iv. provided for the cession of Alsace, excepting Belfort and its district, and German Lorraine with Metz and its district (Pays messin) to the newly constituted German Empire as Reichsland. It was not to be Prussian like the remainder of the Rhineland.

COLLECTIONS OF TREATIES

ANDERSON, FRANK MALLOY. The Constitutions and other Select Documents Illustrative of the History of France. Minneapolis, 1789–1907.

CLERCQ, M. DU. Recueil des traités de la France. Paris, 1852.

HERTSLET, EDWARD, The Map of Europe by Treaty. Vol. iii., 1864–75. London, 1875.

VAST, HENRI. Les Grands Traités du Regne de Louis XIV. (Col. des textes pour l'étude de l'histoire). Paris, 1893.

II.

Main Sources Used for the Narrative

EXCELLENT BIBLIOGRAPHIES FOR SPECIAL PHASES OF THE HISTORY OF ALSACE AND LORRAINE ARE GIVEN IN THE CAMBRIDGE MODERN HISTORY, AND IN THE WORKS OF LAVISSE, DERICHSWEILER, DELAHACHE, ETC. THERE ARE, MOREOVER, MANY ROMANCES, BESIDES VERY VALUABLE ARTICLES TOUCHING THE SUBJECT IN LATE CONTEMPORARY PERIODICAL LITERATURE. THE LIST IS TOO LONG TO BE GIVEN HERE.

ABOUT, EDMOND, F. V. *Alsace*, 1871–'72 Paris, 1873.

BARDOT, GEORGES. *La question des dix villes impériales d'Alsace*. Depuis la paix de Westphalie jusqu'aux arrêts de "réunions" du conseil souverain de Brisack. Paris, 1899.

BRION, M. (Ingénieur-Geographe du Roi.) *Coup d'œil générale sur la France*. Paris, 1720.

A series of maps showing France under every possible aspect. The map showing the jurisdiction of the *Parliaments* and *Superior Councils* has been chosen for its clearness in indicating the extension of the frontier and the policy of centralization.

BRYCE, JAMES—VISCOUNT BRYCE. *The Holy Roman Empire*. London, 1904.

CÆSAR, JULIUS. *De Bella Gallico*.

Cambridge Modern History. Vols. iv., v., viii, and xii. New York, 1906.

COLLIN, CHANOINE. "En Lorraine—La protestation et la Germanisation." *Le Correspondant*, Paris, Nov. 10, 1914.

COXE, WILLIAM. *History of the House of Austria*. 5 volumes. London, 1820.

DERICHSWEILER, HERMANN. *Geschichte Lothringens*. (Der tausendjahrige Kampf um die Westmark.) 2 v. Wiesbaden, 1901.

EMERTON, EPHRAIM. *Medieval Europe*. Boston, 1894.

FISCHER, Jos. S. J. (joint editor). *Cosmographiæ Introductio of Martin Waldseemüller*, in facsimile. New York, 1907.

GODRON, D. A. "Études sur la Lorraine dite Allemande, le Pays messin et l'ancienne province d'Alsace." *Mémoires de la société d'Archéologie de France*. 3e serie, vol. ii., p. 252. Nancy, 1874.

GOETHE, JOHANN WOLFGANG VON. *Wahrheit und Dichtung aus meine Leben.*
GRAD, CHARLES. *Alsace au moment de l'annexion.* Paris, 1872.
GRIESSDORF, JOHANNES. *Der Zug Kaiser Karls V. gegen Metz.* (Hallesche Abhandlungen zur Neueren Geschichte.) Heft 26. Halle, 1891.
GRUCKER, EDUARD. *Die Vogesen.* (Geographische Monographien.) Leipzig, 1908.
HAUSSONVILLE, LE COMTE DE. *Histoire de la réunion de la Loraine à la France.* 4 v. Paris, 1860.
HAUVILLER, DR. ERNST. *Frankreich und Elsass im 17 und 18 Jahrhundert.* Strasburg, 1900.
HINZELIN, EMILE. *Cœurs d'Alsace et de Lorraine.* Paris, 1913.
HOLMES, THOMAS RICE. *Cæsar's Conquest of Gaul.* London, 1899.
KÜRSCHNER'S *Staats-, Hof- und Kommunal-Handbuch.* München, 1913.
LAVISSE, E. *Histoire de France.* Vols. v. to viii. Paris, 1905.
LEGRELLE, ANSÈNE. *Louis XIV. et Strasbourg.* Paris, 1884.
LEPAGE, HENRI. "La Lorraine Allemande, sa réunion à la France son annexation à l'Allemagne." *Mémoires de la Société d'Archéologie Lorraine.* 3e serie, vol. i., p. 255. Nancy, 1873.
—— "Quelques notes sur des peintres Lorrains des XVe, XVIe et XVIIe siècles." *Bulletin de la société d'archéologie Lorraine.* Tome iv., 1853. Nancy.
L'HERMINE, H. DE. *Mémoires de deux voyages et séjours en Alsace.* 1674–76 and 1681. Mulhouse, 1886.
LORENZ, OTTOKAR. *Die Geschichte des Elsasses von Ottokar Lorenz und Wilhelm Scherer.* Berlin, 1886.
METTERNICH, PRINCE RICHARD (editor). *Memoirs of Prince Metternich.* Translated by Mrs. Alexander Napier. New York, 1881.
NORDENSKIOLD, A. E. Facsimile atlas of the most important maps printed in the fifteenth and sixteenth century. Stockholm, 1889.
Ortschafts-Verzeichnis von Elsass-Lothringen. Herausgegeben vom Statistischen Bureau des Kaiserlichen Ministeriums für Elsass-Lothringen. Strasburg, 1907.
PFISTER, CHRISTIAN. "La réunion de l'Alsace à la France." *Revue de Paris,* vol. x., 1900, July, p. 361.
POSCHINGER, HEINRICH VON. *Conversations with Prince Bismarck.* Translated by Sidney Whitman. New York, 1900.
PUTNAM, RUTH. *Charles the Bold.* New York, 1908.
*REUSS, RODOLPHE. *L'Alsace au dix-septième siècle.* Tableau geographique, historique, politique et économique. Paris, 1897. 2 vols.

(This is a most complete and scholarly work, entirely free from the over-zealous partisanship of most literature pertaining to Alsace, yet sympathetic as well as learned.)

SCHÖPFLIN, JOHANN D. *Alsatia illustrata*. Celtica, romana, francia. 2 vols. (vol. i., only in Washington). Colmar, 1751.

STÖBER, AUGUST. *Alsatia*. Issued annually, 1850–1877.

STOUFF, L. "Les possessions Bourguignonnes dans la vallée de Rhin sous Charles le Teméraire." *Annales de l'est*, tome 18.

SYBEL, HEINRICH VON. "Deutschlands Rechte auf Elsass und Lothringen." *Kleine historische Schriften*. Vol. iii., p. 455. Berlin, 1880.

TOUTEY, E. *Charles le Téméraire et la ligue de Constance*. Paris, 1902.

www.ingramcontent.com/pod-product-compliance
Lightning Source LLC
Chambersburg PA
CBHW020427010526
44118CB00010B/467